THE CAGE AND THE M

THE CAGE

AND THE

MIRROR

How to Make Rigid Organizations Resilient Again

by Jeremy McEntire

CAGE & MIRROR PUBLISHING OKLAHOMA CITY

Published by Cage & Mirror Publishing Oklahoma City, Oklahoma cageandmirror.com

ISBN: 979-8-9940343-3-0 (Hardcover / Dust Jacket)
ISBN: 979-8-9940343-0-9 (Hardcover / Casebound)
ISBN: 979-8-9940343-2-3 (Paperback)
ISBN: 979-8-9940343-1-6 (eBook)

First Edition Published in the United States of America

Book cover design by Yasir Nadeem. Cover illustration created with Grok by xAI. Interior design by Vanessa Bruhm. Editing by Maja Vujovic. Text set in Sabon Pro.

For those who see the invisible work.

Table of Contents

On Seeing

I have always looked for the invisible architecture beneath visible behavior. Traffic patterns. Organizational dynamics. The way a single decision propagates through a hierarchy and emerges as something no one intended. I find emergent behavior beautiful the way some people find music beautiful. I cannot help but look for root causes, for the geometry that explains why.

This instinct led me to mathematics, then to software. From writing code to architecting systems to leadership, where processes replace services and abstractions replace people. Across those layers, I noticed the same patterns repeating irrespective of substrate. Code and culture share a physics. How people interact is, to a surprising degree, isomorphic to how objects interact. These equivalences shaped my career.

Within them are antipatterns. Failure modes. Dysfunctions that are computational, financial, and human all at once. I sought to understand them. I read the standard management literature. It offered aspiration. I wanted mechanics.

Reflecting on two decades of building, I recognized a force: inevitable, inescapable, insidious. It manifests differently across systems but produces the same outcome. Compromise. Mediocrity. Apathy.

I call it the Cage, after Weber. It is the natural tendency of organizations to decay through reasonable decisions and good intentions. The force is gravitational. The geometry is unyielding.

But there must be a response.

This is where the Mirror enters. The problem is too systemic for a single solution, too contextual for a checklist. What is required is perspective—the capacity to see your own Cage clearly enough to build deliberately within it.

This book teaches that sight.

A note on evidence. This book relies heavily on first-person observation and narrative. The choice is deliberate. The patterns described here are difficult to see from outside—they must be recognized from within before they can be named. The risk is that personal proximity reads as bias rather than access.

Readers who find the anecdotal structure insufficient should consult the technical papers at cageandmirror. com, where claims are tested against simulations, linguistic analysis, legal scholarship, and formal modeling. The book is designed to create recognition. The papers are designed to survive scrutiny.

Excellence requires variance.

The Cage eliminates variance.

Therefore, the Cage eliminates excellence.

Part I

The Glitch

Patterns That Reveal the Physics

Maps and Territory

E very organization runs on maps—profit-and-loss statements, organizational charts, performance reviews,
strategic frameworks, objectives and key results cascading
from board to team to every individual. These maps
compress reality into something manageable, something
that fits on a slide, something a board can review in under
ninety minutes.

The compression is inevitable, not evil. You cannot
coordinate thousands of people on intuition alone. Scale
demands abstraction, and abstraction requires maps.

Maps always erase something. A street map shows
roads but flattens topography. A subway map shows con-
nections but distorts distance. A profit-and-loss statement
shows revenue and cost but erases the foundational work
that prevents both from collapsing.

The question is whether you remember they are maps.
Whether you know what they erase. Whether you can feel
the moment when optimizing for the map begins destroying
what it represents. And once you see what gets erased,

whether you can build structures that preserve it despite the compression.

Most organizations cannot feel that moment. They optimize for what they measure until the measurements become the purpose. Revenue targets become more real than customers. Velocity metrics become more important than working software. Performance ratings become more significant than actual contribution. The map becomes the territory, and the real territory dies. Quietly. Invisibly.

This book is about the moment you notice the map is lying. The lie comes from geometry: from the information loss inherent in compressing high-dimensional reality into low-dimensional representation, and from the physics of what formal systems can and cannot capture.

Part I shows you that moment four times: the cost center that protects all revenue; the Supervisor who destroys expertise while trying to help; the Go-Getter who gets promoted while the Craftsman goes unrewarded; the engineering team blamed for not fulfilling the promises they never made. These are systematic, predictable consequences of using maps at scale—consequences that persist regardless of management quality. They are glitches, and glitches reveal physics.

You need to see the glitches. You need to feel them. Because once you see and cannot unsee them, you can no longer pretend the maps are complete. Then your real work begins.

CHAPTER 1

The Cost-Center Mirage

There was a team that owned the front door—the edge gateway where every request entered the system. Authentication lived there. Rate limiting. Request routing. The translation layer between external chaos and internal order. The thing that decided whether a request became a transaction or an error code.

A handful of engineers made up the team, nearly all of them new. The IPO had triggered the usual exodus, and the rebuild was still underway. They shipped when they had to, carefully when they could. Their retrospectives were quiet. Their dashboards were green. On the org chart, they were Platform and Shared Services. On the financial statements, they were Technology General and Administrative: a cost center with no revenue attribution, no pipeline contribution, no customer-facing value story.

The business teams building on top of them were profit centers. Those teams had revenue targets, commission structures, customer logos on their slides, and offsite budgets. The platform team received the minimum allocation for team building. Nobody questioned this. It was simply how accounting worked. Teams that had a direct revenue target were profit centers. Those without it were cost centers. Clean lines, clear categories. The map made sense.

The outage was brief. A routine infrastructure update exposed an undocumented dependency lost to institutional knowledge that had walked out the door with the post-IPO departures. The canary deployment ran clean. Production did not. Requests began failing immediately.

The team had monitoring. The team had alerting. The team had rollback procedures they practiced. From first alert to full restoration took only minutes. In those few minutes, more requests failed than in any incident in the company's history. The traffic success graph told the story: flat, then canyon, then flat.

The post-mortem was thorough. The gaps were documented. The procedures were hardened. And something else happened: someone calculated the theoretical maximum exposure, the revenue-at-risk per minute if the API gateway failed during peak traffic. The number appeared in conversations, then in meetings, then in executive decks. The number was sobering.

For a brief period, everyone understood what that team did. Leadership mentioned them. The front door became visible as what it had always been: a multiplicative factor, a defensive moat protecting every dollar the company generated. The platform team represented the smallest budget protecting the largest numbers.

Then quarterly planning started, and their visibility faded. The team took the lesson seriously. They maintained exceptional reliability metrics. They rebuilt critical infrastructure. They deployed capabilities that became foundational to the company's global operations. The company's reliability story, cited in executive presentations, was built on their work.

Their funding decreased anyway. Quarterly budget reviews compressed their resources. Rather than expand to handle the load, the team divested capabilities, shedding responsibilities to maintain operations under pressure. The business teams kept their offsite budgets. The platform team kept the minimum allocation. Their dashboards stayed green, their retrospectives stayed quiet, and their work stayed invisible. Other teams were celebrated for solving problems of their own design. The platform team prevented problems from existing at all. Firefighting is visible. Prevention is not.

I led that team. I left for a place where infrastructure was understood as foundational. The person who replaced me was promoted into the role—he was exactly what the organization wanted. He focused on deliverables, on visible outputs, on the things that appeared in quarterly reviews. When an AWS availability zone failed, he followed the systematic process, accepted the vendor's timelines, waited for the expected resolution. My team had resolved that class of incident in under fifteen minutes. His first recovery took nine hours.

The difference wasn't knowledge or talent. It was that I had pushed the team toward ownership of outcomes rather than compliance with process. That kind of leadership doesn't appear on dashboards. The system couldn't see it, so the system didn't select for it.

On the financial statements, the team remained what they had always been: Technology General and Administrative. A cost center. The map had no field for what it was erasing.

The Accounting Fiction

Legend holds that Tsar Nicholas I, frustrated with engineers debating the railway route between Moscow and Saint Petersburg, took a ruler and drew a straight line across the map. The engineers knew the terrain required accommodation—marshes to avoid, gradients to manage—but the Tsar's line was absolute. They built the railway straight. The map ignored the terrain.

The profit-and-loss statement creates the same problem when mistaken for complete. It compresses reality so that ten thousand people can coordinate without knowing each other; it divides the world into two categories: Revenue and Cost. When a team sells things, they fall into the Profit Center category, and the logic is simple: more salespeople, more sales. These teams get funded and optimized for growth.

A team whose contribution is multiplicative rather than additive falls into a different category. The platform team does not sell the product; they build what the product runs on. But the P&L statement only speaks two languages, and "makes money" is not the label the platform team can claim.

Since they do not generate revenue directly, the system files them under Cost. Once that label sticks, logic takes over. Fiduciary duty says maximize Revenue and minimize Cost, so the rational move is to scrutinize the platform team's headcount, to demand they do more with less. They become akin to the electric bill: necessary, but kept as low as possible.

The P&L statement has a blind spot: no line item exists for silent competence. When the platform team succeeds, nothing happens. The database does not lock up. The API does not time out. The customer notices nothing.

The value is the absence of disaster, and an accounting system built to measure events cannot measure non-events. There is no entry for the outage that did not happen, or for the crisis an engineer quietly prevented six months ago.

The board governs by the map. They see Sales producing visible returns and Platform producing visible expenses, so they make the obvious decision: feed the Profit Center, starve the Cost Center. The P&L statement is a legitimate instrument; the mistake is treating it as complete. Leadership follows the straight line.

When the platform team leaves, they take their knowledge of the terrain with them. Only then does the organization discover what the map could not show.

The Multiplicative Value Problem

Here is what the revenue-at-risk calculation revealed: the platform team, with the smallest budget in Engineering, protected more revenue per dollar spent than any other team in the company. If Marketplace disappeared tomorrow, the company would lose Marketplace revenue. Painful, but bounded. Other products would continue. The platform would route their requests. Customers would still transact. If the platform disappeared tomorrow, everything would stop. Marketplace, Fulfillment, Premium Services—every revenue stream, every customer interaction, every transaction would vanish.

The platform team was *multiplicative* to revenue. It was the coefficient in front of every other team's contribution. But multiplicative value does not fit cleanly into accounting categories designed for additive value. You cannot attribute a multiplier to a single line item. You cannot put "enables all other revenue" into a formula that demands discrete numbers.

So the accounting system does what accounting systems do when faced with something that does not fit: it forces the thing into the nearest available category, even when that category misrepresents its nature. That category is cost center.

The term itself reveals the frame—a thing whose value is measured by its absence, whose success is only defined as spending less. The category was designed for back-of-fice functions whose costs scale linearly with headcount: HR, Finance, Facilities. It was never designed for technical infrastructure that scales with system complexity, where the relationship between input and output is logarithmic rather than linear and a single person's judgment might protect millions in revenue.

But the category exists, and the platform team must go somewhere, so into the cost center box they go. The map cannot represent what they actually do, so the map represents them as something else entirely.

Once the map has spoken, the map's logic takes over. Cost centers should be minimized. Their budgets should be scrutinized. Their headcount should be justified against clear metrics. When cost centers ask for more resources, the default answer is no—they must establish incremental value, prove the ROI, demonstrate why they cannot do this with fewer people.

This is perfectly rational if you believe the map. If the platform team is truly a cost center in the way that Facilities is a cost center, then of course you minimize them. The problem is that the map is lying.

The lie comes from the inevitable information loss when compressing high-dimensional reality into low-dimensional representation. The accounting categories were not designed to capture multiplicative infrastructure value, so they do not capture it. They capture an approximation, a version that looks enough like the truth to be plausible, one that fits into the boxes on the spreadsheet. And that plausible-but-wrong representation becomes the basis for every decision about headcount, budget, and priority.

The Shadow Price of Prevention

The revenue-at-risk calculation revealed something economists call a shadow price—the value of a constraint that does not appear in ordinary accounting. Water looks cheap when it is plentiful. In a drought, its actual value becomes visible; the constraint simply had not bound before. The platform team's value worked the same way. As long as systems ran, as long as requests succeeded, as long as the front door held, nobody paid the price. The seven-minute outage revealed it. For seven minutes, the constraint bound, and the cost became visible.

Shadow prices do not appear continuously. They surface only when the constraint tightens and what was always essential becomes costly because it is missing. The rest of the time they remain theoretical. You can estimate them—revenue per minute multiplied by potential downtime, adjusted for probability of failure—but the estimate feels abstract. In organizations optimizing for quarterly results, abstract risks are discounted heavily against certain costs.

The platform team represented certain costs: salaries, benefits, stock grants, overhead. That cost appeared in every budget review and every headcount discussion. Their value—the shadow price of preventing failure—did not. Prevention's benefit is uncertain; its cost is certain. That asymmetry drives the outcome. Costs are continuous and visible. Preventive value is discontinuous and invisible. Systems that optimize only for what they can see underinvest in prevention because the reduced representation of reality erases the thing that should be optimized.

I understood this. I had seen prevention deferred in favor of features, infrastructure requests denied while product teams expanded, and my budget scrutinized more sharply than initiatives that spent far more and delivered far less. I watched the map misrepresent the territory and capable people accept the map as truth. After five years, I concluded that the problem could not be solved within the existing frame. I left.

The map showed a cost reduction. Salary expense down, headcount target met, cost center minimized. The map was satisfied, but the system became more fragile.

The First Stroke

This is the first stroke of an engine that converts judgment into reflex and mistakes the resulting vibration for progress. The engine runs on maps—necessary, inevitable, indispensable maps that compress reality into manageable representations. But the compression is lossy, and the loss is patterned. The maps preserve what fits into their categories and erase what does not. And because organizations optimize for what they measure, what disappears from the map eventually disappears from the organization.

Judgment resists projection into metrics and falls outside the frame. The map simplifies, and the simplification is not neutral. It favors work that is visible, discrete, and attributable over work that is diffuse, preventive, and multiplicative. And because the map becomes the basis for resource allocation, promotion, and priority, its preferences become the organization's behavior.

The cost-center mirage is the inevitable consequence of using maps that cannot represent certain forms of value. The platform team's value was real; the revenue-at-risk calculation demonstrated that. But the value belonged to a class the representational system could not capture, so the system treated it as if it did not exist. It could only assess it when it no longer existed.

The tragedy was never that the map was wrong—all maps are—but that nobody remembered it was a map. The categories hardened into reality. The cost-center label became the truth. And the people whose work the map erased eventually left for places where different maps might render them visible.

This pattern repeats three more times in the chapters ahead, each time revealing a different dimension of the same underlying physics: formal systems cannot represent everything that matters, and organizations that forget this will destroy the things their maps cannot capture. This is not a fixable bug but a theorem—formal systems unable to account for their own consistency, producing blind spots no amount of leadership skill can eliminate.

CHAPTER 2

The Supervisor's Dilemma

I was working dish return at a college cafeteria during my sophomore year. Plates came down a belt—industrial, relentless, patient in the way that machines are patient. I pulled the plates off, scraped them, stacked them by type, loaded the racks. The work was manual but not mindless. There was a rhythm to it, a flow state you could enter if you arranged things properly.

After a few shifts, I had developed a layout. Three carts positioned in a specific geometry: one for plates, one for bowls and cups, one for silverware and trash. The positioning was not arbitrary. Plates came off the belt, went into the scrape motion, then onto the cart to my left—one motion, no repositioning. Bowls stacked behind me. Silverware forward and right. The layout let me move without thinking, let my hands find the right cart without my eyes leaving the belt. It was flow in the literal sense: continuous motion, minimal cognitive load, maximum throughput.

One evening a supervisor walked over. Nice guy, well-intentioned, the kind of person who genuinely wanted to help. He watched for thirty seconds, maybe forty-five.

Then he said, "Let me help you get organized here." He moved the carts. Plate cart to the right, silverware behind, bowls forward. "There," he said. "Much better. That should make things easier for you." Then he left, satisfied that he had improved things.

My flow collapsed immediately. Each plate now required rediscovery—right hand goes where? Bowls are behind me now? Silverware forward means I turn my back to the belt. The layout that had let me work without thinking now forced me to think about every motion. The belt did not care that I was suddenly thinking instead of moving. It kept running at the same speed it always ran. Plates backed up. I fell behind. The rhythm was gone.

He was not malicious. He had his own map of how a dish station should look, derived from some other station he had supervised, some training he had received, or simply what looked orderly from ten feet away. And he imposed that map onto my work.

He fixed a problem that did not exist by destroying a solution that did. The problem was not my layout. The problem was that my layout did not match his map of what a dish station should look like. His map made sense to him. That was enough to superimpose it over my terrain.

The Map Versus the Work

The manager that redesigns sprint cadence because "two-week sprints are best practice." The director that mandates new ticket taxonomy because "we need consistent labeling across teams." The VP that standardizes interview loops, turning every interview into the same generic script regardless of role or level. None are villains. They are optimizing for what they can see—how work should look—not how work actually flows.

A competent person develops a local solution that works. The solution is contextual, evolved through iteration, shaped by the specific constraints and affordances of that particular work in that particular environment. It may not look optimal to an outside observer because the observer cannot see all the constraints the solution is navigating. The three-cart geometry made sense only if you understood the handedness of the motion, the height of the belt, the speed of the conveyor, the reach distance to each receptacle. From ten feet away, it looked arbitrary.

Someone with broader scope but less context arrives. They see the local solution does not match their mental map of how this kind of work should be organized. So they intervene—not to harm, but to help. To bring order. To impose consistency. To make this station look like the other stations they have seen or read about or imagine in their ideal form. They are helping according to their map, not according to the work.

The local solution is destroyed. Flow replaced by friction. The belt keeps running, oblivious to the fact that the human interface has been degraded. The work gets harder. Throughput drops. Quality suffers, where quality exists to suffer. The supervisor does not see this because they have already moved to the next station, the next improvement, the next opportunity to impose their map onto someone else's practice.

The local damage is invisible from their altitude. What they see is increased consistency, better alignment, standardization successfully deployed.

It is geometry. The Supervisor's map necessarily erases the local details that make the local solution work. The map represents what generalizes across contexts—"dish stations should have this arrangement"—not what particularizes within a context—"this dish station, given these constraints, needs this arrangement."

17

And because the map is the thing that travels up and down the hierarchy—the thing that gets communicated in training and documentation and best practices—it has authority that local practice does not. The map is legible to people three levels removed. Local practice is legible only to the person doing the work.

The Altitude Problem

The higher you are in an organization, the more you depend on maps. You cannot see the work directly. You cannot observe the flow states, the local optimizations, the contextual solutions that make things function. What you see are reports, dashboards, tickets closed, velocity metrics, deployment frequency. You see the shadows that work casts onto measurement systems, not the work itself.

From that altitude, variation looks like inconsistency. Ten teams doing things ten different ways looks like chaos, like lack of standards, like an absence of best practices. The fact that each team has adapted to its local context, has developed practices that work for its specific technical stack and interpersonal dynamics and customer constraints—all of that is invisible. What you see is ten different ticket taxonomies, ten different sprint lengths, ten different deploy processes. And that looks like a problem to be solved.

So you standardize. You pick one approach—usually the one that looks best from your altitude, the one that has the nicest dashboards or the cleanest documentation or the best marketing from its advocates—and you roll it out. Mandate the two-week sprint. Require the standard ticket format. Enforce the uniform deploy process.

And from your altitude, things improve. The dashboards become comparable. The reports are consistent.

You can now roll up metrics across teams, which you could not do before. Your map has improved.

What you cannot see is that three of the ten teams just got significantly worse at their actual work. Their local solutions, the ones adapted to their constraints, have been replaced with a global solution adapted to no one's constraints. They slow down. Friction increases. People start working around the new system because the new system does not fit their reality. But the workarounds are invisible, and the slowdown looks like a temporary adjustment period. And eventually the complaints die down—not because the system started working, but because people learned to game it or circumvent it or simply accepted the new baseline of friction.

The Supervisor's dilemma is that their job requires them to operate from maps, but maps cannot capture the local details that make work effective. They must standardize, because you cannot manage ten teams doing ten different things using ten different mental models. Standardization is how you scale oversight. It erases local optimizations, replaces context-specific solutions with context-free ones, makes some percentage of the work worse. This is not failure. It is the cost of managing at altitude.

The Best Practice Trap

The language of "best practices" obscures what is actually happening. A practice is not best in the abstract. It is best relative to constraints—technical constraints, organizational constraints, team constraints, market constraints.

A practice that is best for a team building greenfield services in a startup is not best for a team maintaining legacy systems under regulatory compliance. A practice that is best for co-located teams with high trust is not best for distributed teams with high turnover. But "best practice" implies universality. It suggests that the practice has been discovered to be optimal across contexts, and that adopting it is simply a matter of discipline and correct deployment.

Organizations accumulate best practices the way they accumulate technical debt—gradually, individually justified, collectively unmanageable. Each best practice made sense to someone at the time it was adopted. Each solved some problem, addressed some gap, brought some improvement. But best practices do not naturally die. They accumulate. And each one adds constraints, adds required behaviors, adds ceremony that made sense in one context but—unchallenged—persists across all of them.

The two-week sprint becomes mandatory even for teams doing exploratory research where two-week cycles make no sense. The five-stage interview loop becomes required even for senior hires who have already demonstrated what the loop is meant to discover. The architectural review board becomes a gate for all changes even for teams that need to move fast and learn from production. Each practice has a constituency—people who genuinely benefited from it, who saw it solve real problems, who advocate for it sincerely. And each constituency defends its practice, ensures it gets encoded in policy, gets embedded in training, gets added to the checklist that new managers inherit.

The result is an ever-thickening layer of process, each piece individually justified, but collectively suffocating. The dish station does not just have one supervisor rearranging the carts. It has five supervisors who have each mandated their own improvement, their own optimization, their own best practice. The carts are now arranged according to a composite map assembled from five different altitudes, none of which can see the actual work, but all of which have authority over the person doing the work.

When the Map Eats the Territory

There comes a point where the gap between the map and the territory becomes so large that the territory simply gives up trying to be itself and starts optimizing for the map instead. The dish station worker stops trying to find flow and starts trying to make the station look like what supervisors expect to see. The engineering team stops optimizing for shipping good software and starts optimizing for metrics that make reports look good. The sales team stops trying to understand customer needs and starts hitting activity targets that someone three levels up decided always correlate with success.

This goes beyond compliance. It is epistemic surrender—the moment when people stop trusting their own judgment about what works and start trusting the map's representation of what should work. When "but this is how we actually do the work" stops being a valid argument against "this is what the process requires." The map has achieved complete authority. The territory has become merely the place where the map's arbitrary instructions get executed.

When you talk to people in this state, they can still tell you how the work actually happens. They know where the workarounds are, which of the steps everyone skips, which requirements everyone treats as theatrics. But they have stopped fighting for the territory. They have accepted that the map is what gets rewarded, what gets measured, what gets career advancement. So they maintain the actual work informally, off-process, and the formal compliance in tickets, reports, and ceremonies.

The system becomes incredibly inefficient. Worse, the territory's knowledge—the accumulated wisdom about what actually works in practice—stops being transmissible. New people learn the map, not the territory. They learn the process, not the practice. They learn how to make

21

the dashboards look right, not how to do the work well. And gradually, over years, the organization forgets how to do the work at all. It only knows how to follow the map. And when the map is wrong—which it inevitably will be—nobody remembers how to navigate by the territory.

The Second Stroke

This is the second stroke of the engine. The accounting map erases prevention. The operational map erases expertise. Both optimize for legibility—for making work visible to people who cannot see the work itself. Both are necessary at scale. You cannot run a large organization without them. But both maps cause the same pathology: they are treated as more authoritative than the reality they represent.

The cost-center mirage erases value that does not fit into accounting categories. The supervisor's dilemma erases knowledge that does not fit into standardized processes. One operates through financial abstraction, the other through operational formulae. The mechanism is the same.

A representation is created to make reality manageable. It simplifies and erases detail. The simplification is treated as an improvement. But decisions made on that basis degrade the territory. The degradation is invisible to people navigating by the map. The cycle continues until the territory collapses or someone notices the abstraction is lying.

The person at the dish station knows it is lying. They can feel it in the additional effort each plate requires, in the loss of rhythm, in the cognitive load that was not there before. But they have no authority to correct it. The map comes from above, encoded in policy, backed by supervisory authority, justified by appeals to consistency, best practices, and scalability. The person doing the work can complain, but the complaint is interpreted as resistance to change, as attachment to old ways, as lack of alignment with organizational improvement.

So they adapt. They work around the new cart arrangement as best they can. They accept the loss of flow as the cost of having a job. Eventually they either internalize the system as correct—"maybe my old way was not better, maybe I was just attached to it"—or they leave for somewhere else where they hope the abstractions might be less divorced from the territory.

The Supervisor never knows which outcome occurred. From their altitude, the dish station looks better organized now. The carts are arranged properly. The improvement has been implemented.

CHAPTER 3

The Go-Getter Fallacy

The CEO wanted go-getters. People who took initiative. Who saw problems and fixed them. Who did not wait to be told what to do. He said this in all-hands meetings, in leadership offsites, in the company values deck that got presented to new hires. The company valued people who drove change, who raised the bar, who had impact beyond their immediate role.

This was not empty rhetoric. He meant it. The performance review template had a section specifically for "initiative and leadership." Promotions explicitly required demonstrating influence outside your core responsibilities.

He meant well. What he built was a culture where the loudest people got promoted and the best people got overlooked.

The Janitor and the Go-Getter

There was a Janitor who had been at the company longer than most of the engineers. He was the best janitor I have ever seen. Not because he cleaned faster or worked longer hours, but because he had learned the building.

He knew which conference rooms accumulated the most mess after all-hands meetings and needed extra attention. He knew which restrooms ran out of supplies first and in what order to restock them so he was never caught short during the afternoon rush. He knew the exact time to refill the coffee stations so that the three-PM slump would not hit empty pots. He had optimized his routes through the building to minimize backtracking, had negotiated relationships with the loading dock staff so supplies arrived when he needed them, and had developed a sense for which spaces were about to become problems before they actually became problems.

Nobody celebrated him. No shout-outs in all-hands. No spotlight in the weekly newsletter. No manager asking him to present his methods to the new Facilities hires. He had mastered his role, and mastery—when quiet—is invisible. His work manifested as the absence of complaints, the consistent presence of supplies, the fact that the building simply worked. People walked into clean restrooms and found soap and paper towels and never thought about the system that ensured those things were there. The executive team had their morning coffee and never wondered why the pots were always full at seven forty-five.

Then there was the Go-Getter. He was also in Facilities, nominally at the same level, hired around the same time. He was always visible. Popping into meetings he was not invited to. Volunteering for cross-functional committees. Organizing team-building events that fizzled. Taking on projects that sounded impressive in planning—"renegotiate vendor contracts"; "implement new inventory system"—but that either shipped late and underperformed or quietly got deprioritized and forgotten.

His day-to-day work was adequate. He was visible. He had opinions about company strategy that he shared in Slack channels. He wrote memos about process improvements that occasionally got forwarded up the chain. He was always raising his hand.

Over fifteen years, the Janitor had never been promoted. Within eighteen months, the Go-Getter had been promoted twice. First to a lead role coordinating schedules across Facilities staff, then to a managerial role overseeing multiple buildings.

The Janitor retired. At his retirement party, someone gave a short speech about his dedication and consistency. People clapped politely. He left with a plaque and a gift card.

Three months after he retired, the coffee situation degraded noticeably. The afternoon rush started hitting empty pots. Conference rooms after big meetings stayed messy longer. Restroom supplies ran out at unpredictable times. It was small things, none catastrophic, but the building stopped working as smoothly as it used to. Nobody connected it to the Janitor's absence.

The problems were too diffuse, too distributed across time and space. The Go-Getter—now a manager—commissioned a review of Facilities processes to identify inefficiencies. The review recommended better inventory tracking and more systematic scheduling. Both sounded reasonable. Neither addressed the missing variable—the accumulated judgment of someone who had learned the system at a level of granularity that no process document would ever capture.

The Optics Premium

You can become the world's best at your actual job—learning every edge case, developing judgment that saves the company from mistakes they will never know they almost made, building expertise that compounds over years into something irreplaceable. Or you can be seen working on cross-functional projects, "driving alignment"; "raising the bar"; "influencing without authority." Both methods require effort. One builds the product; the other builds a career.

The site reliability engineer whose systems never break—dashboards green, alerts silent, uptime at five nines—faces promotion time with "We need to see more impact." The infrastructure was not broken, so what did you actually do? The answer ("I prevented it from breaking, through careful design, proactive monitoring, and accumulated knowledge of failure modes") does not translate into the language of impact. Impact requires visibility. Prevention is invisible.

The pattern repeats. The designer whose products are so intuitive users never get confused loses promotions to whoever shipped the flashy redesign that generated buzz. The technical writer whose documentation cuts onboarding time in half loses to whoever extracted the library and gave the conference talk. Craft is invisible. Performance is not.

The system cannot ask different questions for different kinds of work without becoming unmanageable. Performance reviews must be comparable across people, roles, and teams. Comparability requires standardization. Standardization requires common metrics. Common metrics require reducing all work to a small set of dimensions: impact, scope, complexity, leadership.

That reduction is lossy. Craft, prevention, maintenance, and judgment fall outside the template—they are the invisible infrastructure that makes all the visible work possible.

The asymmetry is architectural. Formal systems record events: projects shipped, presentations delivered, initiatives launched, problems visibly solved. Events are discrete, countable, attributable. They fit naturally into performance reviews because performance reviews sample accomplishments, and accomplishments are events.

The craftsman does not produce events. The craftsman produces state—a continuous condition of accumulated knowledge, maintained quality, deepening expertise.

You cannot point to the moment the Janitor became expert in the building's systems. There was no single event. The expertise accrued gradually, through thousands of small observations that left no artifact. The state exists, but the measurement system has no mechanism to capture it.

This is not a flaw in how evaluators think. It is a structural limitation of what formal systems can represent. Performance reviews ask: what did you accomplish? The question presupposes events. The craftsman's answer—"I maintained a state of deep knowledge that prevented problems you never saw"—does not parse. The Go-Getter's answer—"I launched three initiatives and presented to the executive team twice"—parses immediately. Events. Discrete. Countable. The measurement determines the visibility. The visibility determines the reward. The reward determines behavior.

The Go-Getter's Actual Record

Examined closely, the Go-Getter's record is mixed. The vendor renegotiation saved money on paper but degraded service quality in ways that only became apparent six months later. The new inventory system shipped but was so cumbersome that people worked around it, entering data in batches once a week to satisfy reporting requirements while maintaining their own spreadsheets for actual operations. The cross-functional committee he chaired produced a strategic framework document that was presented to executives, praised for its comprehensiveness, and then quietly shelved because implementing it would require coordination that nobody had capacity for.

None of this appeared in his performance review. The vendor renegotiation showed cost savings in the first quarter. The inventory system showed up as a completed project. The strategic framework was cited as evidence of leadership and strategic thinking. By the time the second-order consequences became apparent (degraded service, workarounds, shelfware), he had already been promoted. The problems were inherited by whoever came after him, absorbed into the general background dysfunction that every organization tolerates, or papered over by the people doing actual work who quietly compensated for the gaps.

The system has no memory for second-order consequences. It evaluates what is visible at the time of evaluation. First-order effects are visible: project shipped, cost reduced, framework delivered. Second-order effects (service degraded, workarounds proliferated, coordination failed) appear later, diffusely, often in parts of the organization distant from where the original initiative occurred.

And even when they appear, they are rarely traced back to their cause. The organization does not run counterfactuals. It does not ask: what would have happened if we had not renegotiated that vendor contract? It only sees: vendor costs went down, therefore initiative succeeded.

The craftsman's work has the opposite temporal signature. First-order effects are invisible: nothing broke, supplies were present, coffee was ready. Second-order effects compound over years: new hires ramp up faster because documentation is clear; incidents decrease because prevention is embedded in design; the building runs smoothly because someone learned its rhythms.

But performance systems do not measure compounding second-order effects. They measure discrete first-order accomplishments. So the system misvalues the work that creates long-term compounding value, in favor of work that creates short-term visible wins.

The Culture This Creates

A culture that rewards go-getters over craftsmen runs a selection algorithm on its entire workforce, favoring visibility over substance and breadth over depth. Once running, it becomes self-reinforcing.

People observe who gets promoted. The person who mastered the craft stays at the same level while the committee volunteer moves up. Depth of expertise matters less than breadth of visibility. They adjust: better to be adequate at the core role and spend surplus energy on visible initiatives—writing the blog post rather than refining the system, giving the talk rather than preventing the failure.

Over time, the organization's expertise distribution shifts. The average level of craft declines gradually as people who would have been the next generation of experts choose breadth over depth. The organization becomes shallower. And because expertise is often invisible until its absence causes catastrophic failure, the degradation goes unnoticed until something breaks that should not have been allowed to break.

Meanwhile, the people who do still choose craft become increasingly frustrated. They see less competent but more visible people getting promoted over them. Eventually, many leave. The organization loses exactly the people it most needs and retains exactly the people who are best at gaming the performance system.

The CEO genuinely wanted initiative and leadership. But the mechanism—the performance template, the promotion criteria, the visibility bias built into how accomplishment is measured—selects for noise over signal, theater over substance, breadth over depth.

The pattern scales. General Electric under Jack Welch became the most celebrated case study in American business—a company that rewarded bold moves, ranked and culled relentlessly, optimized for quarterly performance with mechanical precision. The business press lionized Welch for two decades.

What the coverage missed was the infrastructure decay happening beneath the growth story. The institutional knowledge that kept turbines running and financial services sound was being systematically culled alongside the "bottom performers." The go-getter culture Welch built selected for visibility at every level: executives who hit targets and told compelling stories rose; engineers and operators who quietly maintained capability did not.

When Jeffrey Immelt inherited the company, he inherited a system that looked strong on metrics and was rotting underneath. The consequences took fifteen years to become fully visible. By 2018, GE had lost over eighty percent of its market value and was removed from the Dow Jones Industrial Average—the last original member, finally culled by the logic it had championed.

The Third Stroke

This is the third stroke of the engine. Accounting erases prevention. Operations erases expertise. Performance erases craft. Each optimized for legibility—for making work visible to evaluators who cannot directly observe the work itself.

The cost-center mirage erased the value of what did not go wrong. The supervisor's dilemma erased the knowledge embedded in local practice. The Go-Getter fallacy erased the mastery that compounds over years. Three domains, three mechanisms, one underlying geometry: formal systems compress reality to make it manageable.

The compression is lossy. What gets lost are the dimensions that do not fit the compression schema. And because organizations make decisions based on the compressed representation, they systematically destroy what their maps cannot capture.

The Janitor knew the building. That knowledge had value—real, measurable value that became visible only after he left and the building's operations degraded. But the knowledge was of a type that performance systems cannot represent. It was an accumulated state, a gradually built expertise, a lived relationship with a complex system. The performance template had no box for that, so it treated the knowledge as if it did not exist. And the organization, navigating by the template, made the rational decision: promote the visible person, let the quiet person retire at the same level he entered.

Years later, when the building runs less smoothly, when small inefficiencies have compounded into noticeable dysfunction, nobody will trace it back to that decision. The causal chain is too long, too diffuse, too confounded by other changes. The organization will not learn that it made an error.

It will commission a process review, implement new tracking systems, hire consultants to optimize Facilities operations. All of which might help marginally, but none of which will replace what was lost: the judgment that comes from years of attention, the expertise that comes from caring about craft, the knowledge that accrues when someone masters a domain rather than performing only adequately while seeking visibility elsewhere.

The engine keeps running. The maps keep erasing reality. The territory keeps degrading. The people operating the engine—the CEO who wanted go-getters, the managers designing performance templates, the evaluators making promotion decisions—they mean well. They are trying to reward excellence, to identify leadership, to advance the right people. They are simply navigating by maps that cannot represent the terrain. And the maps, being simpler and more legible than the terrain, win.

Three strokes. Three domains. The fourth operates where all the others converge.

CHAPTER 4

The Engineering Trap

When Timelines Trump Truth

Marketing wants something to say this quarter. Sales wants something to close this month. Finance wants growth that makes the line go up smoothly, without the volatility that spooks investors. Engineering is handed impossible timelines, excluded from scoping conversations, then blamed when the product ships broken.

The Asynchronous Lie

Marketing and development do not have to run on the same timeline. They are asynchronous by nature. Marketing operates in narrative time: quarters, campaigns, keynotes, fiscal cycles that align with board meetings and earnings calls and the rhythm of investor expectations. Engineering operates in discovery time: unknown unknowns, emergent complexity, systems integration, the irreducible duration required to learn what you do not yet know you need to learn.

Every organization synchronizes them anyway. Marketing needs something to announce at the user conference in Q3, Sales needs a feature to close the enterprise deal, Finance needs the revenue accrual that depends on delivery, the board needs guidance that shows continued growth. So Engineering inherits Marketing's timeline because financial necessity overrides technical soundness.

The pattern is consistent across companies, industries, and decades. Business designs the thing: feature set, pricing model, market positioning, competitive differentiation. Sales sells it before it exists, before Engineering has seen the requirements, before anyone has assessed feasibility. Marketing announces it: keynote presentation, press release, customer roadmap, promises encoded in contracts and earnings guidance. Engineering inherits the timeline: ship by Q3. We already told customers, the revenue is in the forecast, the board has been briefed.

Then comes ruthless prioritization. The scope that was promised cannot be delivered in the time available, so cut features. Ship the minimum that satisfies the promise, or the minimum that can be defended as satisfying it if you squint and avoid testing the edges. The promise is always the same: fix it later, add the missing pieces in the next release, address the technical debt after launch—hopeful projections, genuine intentions from people who have not yet learned that "later" never comes because the next quarter's cycle has already begun.

So Engineering enters heroic mode: nights, weekends, skipped meals, deferred maintenance. Technical debt accumulates, the corrosive kind, born from insufficient time rather than strategic tradeoffs. The system ships at seventy percent quality, delivering eighty percent of what was promised. Customers are unimpressed. Adoption is slower than projected. Support tickets pile up. The sales team quietly stops leading with the new feature. Marketing shifts focus to the next announcement.

When the post-mortem happens (and it always happens, because missing targets triggers scrutiny), the framing is always the same: Engineering failed to deliver what business needed when business needed it. Engineering is blamed for not being scrappy enough, for misunderstanding urgency, for gold-plating when simplicity was called for.

The Stereotype Trap

We talk about diversity and inclusion, about how wrong it is to stereotype people based on identity, to assume what you are capable of doing based on who you are. But stereotypes about engineers are taken for granted. Business-wise, they do not get it. They do not understand product, revenue, sales, or the customer. They are too focused on technical elegance. They do not appreciate urgency. They need to be more scrappy, more pragmatic, more willing to make tradeoffs.

These characterizations are presented as observations, as professional assessments, as the unfortunate but necessary truth about how engineers are. Because these portrayals are framed as professional rather than personal, they are immune to the diversity-and-inclusion frameworks that would question them in other contexts. Nobody says "engineers are genetically predisposed to miss deadlines." They say "engineering culture tends toward perfectionism at the expense of pragmatism," which sounds measured and reasonable while invoking the same stereotype.

The Engineer who says "this timeline is technically impossible" is heard as "we are not scrappy enough." The timeline was set by Marketing six weeks ago. It was encoded in the earnings call last quarter. It is in contracts that have been signed. The timeline is not negotiable, so the Engineer's protest is interpreted as psychological resistance—as unwillingness to do what is necessary, as lack of customer focus, as failure to understand that perfect is the enemy of good.

The Engineer protests because their team has lived the cycle—promised time to fix it later, only to watch "later" deferred until technical debt becomes load-bearing and unmaintainable. They know that shipping a broken tool is self-sabotage, because the support overhead and customer churn will cost more than the delay would have.

This knowledge has no authority. The protest runs into Marketing's announced launch date, Sales' promised delivery timeline, Finance's committed revenue guidance, the CEO's scheduled keynote. Local knowledge fights global commitments. Local knowledge loses. The new system ships broken, and the engineers are blamed for not making it work within the constraints they were given.

The Pattern That Repeats

The 737 MAX was Boeing's response to Airbus competition—a fuel-efficient update to a proven airframe, designed to require minimal pilot retraining, so airlines could slot it into existing fleets without costly certification delays. Engineering knew the aerodynamic changes created handling problems at certain attitudes. They designed a software system, MCAS (Maneuvering Characteristics Augmentation System), to compensate. They also knew MCAS had failure modes that could be catastrophic if pilots did not understand what was happening.

The timeline did not permit extensive pilot training. Training would slow certification. Slower certification would delay deliveries. Delayed deliveries would lose orders to Airbus. So the training was minimized, the documentation was sparse, and the software that could point the nose down without pilot input was not emphasized in the materials that pilots received.

The engineers had flagged the risks. The timeline absorbed the flags. Three hundred forty-six people died in two crashes eighteen months apart. The pattern is identical to every other case: business designed it; Sales sold it; Marketing positioned it against the main rival Airbus; Engineering inherited a timeline that assumed away the hard problems. When the consequences became visible, the framing was about software failures and pilot error—not about the system that made those failures inevitable.

The gaming industry compresses the same pattern into shorter cycles. Cyberpunk 2077 was announced in 2012, promised repeatedly, delayed multiple times, and still shipped broken in December 2020 because the marketing apparatus simply could not stop. CD Projekt Red's engineers knew the game was not ready. They worked anyway—extended overtime burned through the team for months.

The launch was catastrophic: game-breaking bugs, missing features, performance so poor on base consoles that Sony pulled it from the PlayStation Store. The studio's reputation, built over years on The Witcher series, was damaged in a week. The developers had known. Their protests were absorbed by the timeline, which was set by investor expectations, marketing commitments, and holiday sales windows that engineering had no authority to move.

Enterprise software lives in this pattern so continuously that practitioners stop noticing it. The sales team demos a product that does not exist to close a seven-figure deal. The contract specifies delivery in six months. Engineering learns about the commitment after the signature. The requirements assume capabilities the platform does not have. The timeline assumes development velocity the team has never achieved. So Engineering enters heroic mode, cuts scope, builds workarounds, ships something that technically satisfies the contract while failing to deliver what the customer actually needed. The customer is dissatisfied. The support burden is enormous. The sales team has moved on to the next deal. The engineers who warned that the timeline was impossible are blamed for not being scrappy enough.

Medical devices compress the pattern around periodic regulatory windows. FDA approval timelines create hard deadlines that do not flex for technical reality. A device that misses its approval window may wait months or years for the next review cycle. The commercial pressure to hit the looming window overrides engineering caution.

Corners are cut—sometimes in testing, sometimes in documentation, sometimes in the device itself. Some shortcuts only get caught in post-market surveillance: recalls, warning letters, consent decrees. Most flaws do not surface until the consequences compound into patient harm that finally triggers scrutiny. The engineers knew. Their concerns were noted, documented, and overridden by the timeline. When the FDA issues its warning letter, the framing is about quality system failures—not about the system that made quality failures inevitable.

These examples span aerospace, gaming, enterprise software, and medical devices. These industries share nothing except the pattern. Business sets the timeline. Sales sells to the timeline. Marketing announces the timeline. Engineering inherits the gap between what was promised and what is possible. The gap becomes technical debt, quality shortcuts, deferred maintenance, or catastrophic failure—depending on how large the gap was and how much luck intervened. When consequences become visible, Engineering is blamed for not being scrappy enough, for gold-plating, for failing to embrace minimum viable thinking. The system that created the gap escapes scrutiny because the system is everyone's context and no one's responsibility.

Mode A Versus Mode B

Mode A sells before building, promises before knowing, announces before achieving. It optimizes for the smoothness of the narrative, for the continuity of the growth story, for the investor confidence that comes from hitting guidance estimates. It values heroic recoveries over preventive design, visible shipping over invisible quality, marketing alignment over engineering reality. Mode A produces timelines and commitments—announcements that precede capability. It does not reliably produce working software.

Mode B builds before selling, knows before promising, achieves before announcing. It optimizes for product truth over narrative continuity, for actual capability over speculated potential, for the compounding advantage of shipping things that work rather than the short-term optics of shipping things on time. Mode B produces breakthroughs, surprises, moments when a product exceeds expectations because the expectations were set by reality rather than by aspiration.

Apple's privacy stance is Mode B. It was developed over years, with careful attention to both the technical implementation and the legal positioning, and it was announced only when it was genuinely defensible. The result is a moat that competitors cannot easily replicate, a market position that creates real differentiation, a technical capability that actually works rather than one that sounds good in slides. Privacy succeeded because it was protected from Mode A's timeline pressure, because it was allowed to be ready before it was required to be visible.

Privacy is the exception. Most of Apple's recent product history is Mode A: Vision Pro polished but not ready, Apple Intelligence promised but not delivered, Siri stagnating under the weight of commitments made faster than its capabilities developed. Apple is simply the most visible example of a pattern that affects every company operating under quarterly scrutiny and every engineering team working inside a system that optimizes for demonstrable progress over actual progress.

The Soul Ache

Engineers living inside this system see exactly how the product was made broken—through a process that refused to allow success. They see the corners that were cut because there was no time, the technical debt incurred because missing the deadline was not an option, the edge cases that were not tested, the failure modes that were not addressed, the scale problems that were deferred, the integration issues that were worked around instead of solved.

When customers encounter these problems, blame flows downhill to Engineering. The business team that designed something technically impossible escapes scrutiny, as does the sales team who sold it before it existed, the marketing team who announced it on a timeline that violated physics. Engineering is blamed because the system's narrative requires an accountable party and when it comes to execution, Engineering is the accountable party.

The promises being made right now—"we will fix it later"; "we will address the technical debt in the next cycle"; "we will add the missing features after launch"— are commitments the system cannot keep because it is already generating the next cycle's commitments, the next quarter's revenue targets, the next announcement that will consume whatever capacity might have been available for remediation.

So engineers work nights and weekends trying to deliver something that will not completely embarrass the company. They cut scope ruthlessly, prioritizing the features that demo well over the features that matter for actual use. They write code they know is fragile, that will break under conditions they can predict but do not have time to prevent. They ship, watch the early reviews, and feel the specific ache that comes from knowing they could have done better if the system had allowed it.

The burnout that follows is specific: it comes from being set up to fail, from being blamed for failures encoded in the constraints they inherited, from watching the cycle repeat quarter after quarter. Meanwhile, the people setting the timelines learn nothing because the system's feedback loops do not connect their decisions to the consequences.

YAGNI, KISS, MVP

The engineering aphorisms that are supposed to represent wisdom—YAGNI (You Aren't Gonna Need It), KISS (Keep It Simple Stupid), MVP (Minimum Viable Product)—have been weaponized into Mode A's defense mechanisms. When engineers protest that the timeline is impossible, the response is "YAGNI; do not gold-plate it; ship the minimum." When engineers say the architecture will not scale, the response is "KISS; do not over-engineer; solve today's problem." When engineers warn about edge cases, the response is "MVP, ship something and iterate."

These aphorisms were originally about focus, about avoiding speculative complexity, about learning from users rather than building in a vacuum. They have been repurposed into justifications for shipping broken software.

YAGNI becomes "do not build the error handling you will definitely need." KISS becomes "do not design for the scale you will definitely hit." MVP becomes "ship something that barely works and call it iteration."

The aphorisms survive because they are directionally correct in the abstract. You should not build features nobody needs. You should not introduce complexity that does not pay for itself. You should ship early and learn from reality. But the aphorisms have been evacuated of their original context and deployed as all-purpose responses to engineering concerns, as rhetorical weapons that allow business stakeholders to dismiss technical reality without engaging with it.

When an engineer says "this will break at scale," the response "do not over-engineer it" is a dismissal. It takes an aphorism designed to prevent one kind of error—speculative complexity—and uses it to enforce a different kind of error: ignoring predictable failure modes. Because the aphorism sounds like engineering wisdom, because it is phrased in engineering language, the dismissal feels like it comes from engineering values rather than being imposed on engineering from outside.

This is the final inversion. Engineers are blamed for shipping broken software under impossible timelines using their own language, their own values, their own professional identity. The failure is framed as "Engineering failed to be scrappy enough, failed to embrace MVP thinking, failed to keep it simple." The Mode A pathology is attributed to engineering culture rather than to the system that constrains engineering. And engineers, already demoralized by the development cycle, internalize the blame.

Why This Is the Cage

This is the Fiduciary Trap. Public companies provide earnings guidance, that guidance becomes commitment, and missed commitments trigger exactly the scrutiny directors are legally obligated to avoid. So timelines are set by financial necessity, not technical reality. Engineering inherits that gap.

A smooth line of incremental progress is defensible. A jagged line, with occasional large bets and visible setbacks, is not, even when the jagged line leads somewhere better. The system selects for predictable mediocrity over unpredictable excellence.

Every function operates in its own time: Marketing in narrative time, Finance in quarterly time, Sales in pipeline time. Execution is where these disparate timelines converge. The gap between commitment and capability becomes visible only at execution. Visibility requires accountability. Engineering executes. Engineering gets the blame.

The Cage is not built by bad actors. It is built by reasonable people following reasonable rules that produce unreasonable outcomes.

The Fourth Stroke

This is the fourth stroke of the engine. Accounting erases prevention. Operations erases expertise. Performance erases craft. Timelines erase possibility itself—the possibility of shipping only when ready, of building before selling, of knowing before promising, of doing the work properly instead of heroically recovering from self-inflicted wounds.

The pattern is complete. Across four domains—finance, operations, performance management, product development—the geometry is the same. Formal systems compress reality into maps. The maps are necessary but incomplete. Organizations optimize for what the maps capture. What the maps cannot capture gets systematically destroyed. The people operating inside the system—the CFO trying to provide guidance, the director trying to standardize processes, the manager trying to identify high performers, the product lead trying to ship on schedule—they are all navigating by maps that erase the things they need most.

The platform team lost funding because the accounting map could not represent multiplicative value. The dish station worker's flow was destroyed because the operational map could not represent local expertise. The Janitor retired invisible because the performance map could not reveal accumulated craft. Engineers burn out and leave because the timeline map cannot represent the irreducible duration required to build things properly.

The losses are systematic. The platform team's funding, the dish station worker's flow, the Janitor's accumulated craft, the engineers burning out under impossible timelines—each appears local, an individual departure, an unfortunate outcome. The pattern says otherwise. Incomplete maps, treated as complete, produce these losses reliably.

You have seen the glitches. Now see where they come from.

The Tragedy of Process

We've built engines that convert reflex into motion, machines that shake instead of move, that call their noise productivity and their complacency balance.

Act I: The Engine Starts

Every living craft begins as a conversation between judgment and necessity. Someone sees clearly, acts precisely, and then teaches what they've learned so others don't have to rediscover it the hard way. Process is born in that moment—not as dogma, but as memory. It is the handwriting of wisdom.

Toyota's just-in-time did not appear because a consultant loved kanban cards; it appeared because Taiichi Ohno watched how supermarkets restocked: pull, not push; demand, not doctrine. The Agile Manifesto wasn't born to fuel certification mills; it was a small rebellion by engineers tired of lying to Gantt charts. Great processes began as humane instruments, tuned to reality by people who cared more about truth than ceremony.

But memory is seductive. To spread a craft, we compress judgment into steps. To scale it, we strip away context. To protect the novice, we sand off the edges where danger and discovery live together. We reduce the living to the repeatable. Somewhere in that well-intended compression, the script quietly supplants the substance.

The engine starts.

The cadence is reassuring: ka-chunk, ka-chunk. Each stroke converts "why" into "how"; each rotation swaps local discernment for general instruction. At first, the machine magnifies what we already know. Then it keeps turning even when the world has moved on.

What began as the memory of insight becomes the imitation of form. We aren't repeating the masters; we're parroting their gestures—beautifully, confidently, out of time.

Act II: The Illusion of Motion

Step into the cockpit of a modern organization. Dashboards glow. Velocity graphs climb. OKRs gleam a pleasing shade of green. Net Promoter Scores nudge upward with statistical significance. Slack hums. Tickets close. Sprints complete. Five stars light the dashboard.

From inside the glass, it feels like speed.

But the dials do not measure direction. They measure vibration.

A team doubles "story points" by redefining "done." A product hits its activation metric because the funnel moved the definition of "active." Operations "reduce incidents" by recategorizing failures as "known exceptions." The survey average sits at 4.5 of 5 and we cheer as if excellence had been achieved, forgetting that our culture now treats five stars as the default tap from indifferent thumbs. Complacency wears the medal that once belonged to mastery.

That is the quiet duality of five stars. Once, that fifth star meant delight. Now it often means "did not annoy me." On the delivery side, teams wave the same five as proof of excellence; on the user side, customers click it because anything less feels like punishment. We have redefined success downward. "Acceptable" now masquerades as "great," and the inflation is so universal that few remember the exchange rate.

None of this is malicious. It is what happens when measures become targets. We elevate what we can count because counting feels like control. And because we fear ambiguity, we mistake more measurement for more truth. We polish the glass until it shines too brightly to see through.

We think we are flying. We are idling at full throttle.

Act III: The Compression

Anxiety doesn't love silence, so we tighten the cycle.

Sprints shorten. Pivots multiply. "Transformation" follows transformation, each new initiative correcting the last. We oscillate between "empower the teams" and "tighten the controls," between "move fast" and "measure twice," between "innovate" and "stabilize"—ka-chunk, ka-chunk—until the swings blur into a single quake.

Picture the leadership offsite. Monday morning opens with a keynote: "We must move faster—customer expectations have changed." By Monday afternoon, the breakout session reviews last quarter's failures and concludes: "We must slow down and get it right." Tuesday's action items include both "accelerate deployment cycles" and "add additional review gates." No one notices the contradiction because both feel urgent. The calendar fills. The engine spins faster. Yet nothing moves.

At this speed, opposites coexist.

The same company that mandates Six Sigma precision also demands "hacker speed." The same quarter that prizes psychological safety penalizes dissent. The same roadmap that chants "customer-obsessed" ignores the customer's plea to stop adding half-working features and make the product reliable. Order and chaos declare themselves rival schools, but both are reflexes of the same engine. We have mistaken the vibration for virtue.

When the oscillation accelerates far enough, it creates an illusion of bifurcation. The organization feels split into two camps—each convinced the other is the problem— when in truth both are artifacts of a system that shakes so constantly it can no longer tell motion from movement. The extremes appear simultaneous because the engine never rests long enough to settle.

We mistake velocity for progress and ignore direction entirely.

In this compression, "learning" becomes avoiding yes-terday's pain at all costs. Twain's stove cat wouldn't sit on a hot stove again. It wouldn't sit on a cold one either. Process—once a memory of intelligence—calcifies into a phobia of variance. We overlearn. We stop experimenting where it matters and over-experiment where it doesn't. We change the ceremony when the structure is wrong. We optimize the surface and forget the source.

The result isn't balance. It is motion sickness.

Act IV: The Avoidance

Why do we keep spinning the engine when the noise is deafening? Because the tremor is comforting. It tells us we're "doing something." It spares us the terrifying work of pausing long enough to wonder whether we're pointed anywhere at all.

Modern institutions have learned to manage anxiety at scale. When something feels wrong, we add a metric. When the metric reveals discomfort, we add a program. When the program sputters, we add another survey. We regulate the symptoms of our fear—of failure, of blame, of uncertainty—until the meta-process is louder than the work itself. The company spends more energy measuring engagement than engaging, more cycles proving "alignment" than choosing a direction.

But the system requires operators. We are all complicit.

The individual contributor knows the process is wasteful but follows it because "that's how we do things here." To deviate is to invite scrutiny. To comply is to be invisible. Safety lies in following the script, even when the script is nonsense.

The middle manager administers the engagement survey she knows is theater because challenging it upward feels riskier than administering it downward. She has learned that proposing to remove process is career-limiting, while adding process—even bad process—signals initiative. So she adds her stroke. Ka-chunk.

The executive demands "data-driven decisions" not because data illuminates, but because data diffuses accountability. If the decision fails, the data was wrong. If it succeeds, the framework was sound. Judgment is dangerous; process is safe. So he commissions more dashboards, more studies, and mistakes the growing stack of analysis for progress toward clarity.

None of us is the villain. We are participants in a system that has optimized for the appearance of rigor over the practice of it. We have built a self-regulating anxiety machine, and we feed it because silence feels like failure.

Consider the five-star mirage again. In many systems, five is the default, four is an insult, and three is a quiet death sentence. Internally, the corollary is the nine-out-of-ten performance review executives expect as the baseline signal of "healthy." A nine becomes average. A ten is obligatory. Anything less implies crisis. With the scale rigged at the top, mediocrity looks like mastery and real mastery becomes mathematically invisible. We aren't celebrating excellence; we've hidden the yardstick for it.

We do not see the system; we treat the side effects. We are not steering; we are soothing.

The tragedy is not intentional. Most leaders genuinely believe process is the Right Way. It feels moral, safe, fair. But that faith smuggles in a presumption: that no other way could be as good or better. When process becomes morality, curiosity becomes heresy. We stop fixing what is broken because the dashboard says it isn't. We fix what is working because the ritual says it must look a certain way.

Guardrails exist to keep novices from catastrophe. Rails exist to keep trains obedient. We have mistaken one for the other.

We tell ourselves we've eliminated failure. Often we have only redefined it. We tell ourselves we've improved quality. Often we have only trimmed the tails of the distribution—the worst and the best—until everything sits neatly under the curve where it can be insured, explained, and applauded. We wanted fairness; we achieved flatness.

And with flatness comes the quiet death of optionality. The conditions that allow exceptionality to matter are engineered away—not because anyone planned to kill them, but because they don't graph well on the quarterly board deck.

Act V: The Recognition

The engine is not evil. It is mindless. What began as wisdom made visible has become wisdom made impossible.

We see this. We are not fools. We know the survey is theater, the metric will be gamed, the process wastes more than it saves. We participate anyway. We add our stroke—ka-chunk—because the alternative is silence, and silence feels like failure.

But the silence is not failure. The silence is where you hear what the work actually needs.

The engine is loud enough to drown out everything else. It fills the room with the sound of doing, the comfort of motion, the reassurance that something is happening even when nothing moves. The noise obscures questions we are afraid to ask: whether the process remembers what it was born to protect, whether the metric measures what matters or merely what's countable, whether the guardrail has become a rail. These questions require judgment—the thing the engine was built to preserve and has learned to replace.

The tragedy is not that the engine runs. Engines run; that is what engines do. The tragedy is that we have forgotten we built it. We feed it. We mistake its rhythm for our heartbeat. We keep adding strokes—ka-chunk, ka-chunk—because stopping feels like dying.

Somewhere beneath the noise, the work is waiting. It has always been waiting.

There is a difference between the hum of avoidance and the quiet of orientation. One fills the room so nothing else can be heard. The other opens space for questions that matter. You cannot find that quiet by adding another metric, another process, another transformation initiative. You find it only by letting the engine idle long enough to hear what it has been drowning out.

We have built machines that shake instead of move, that call their noise productivity and their complacency balance.

The work is still there, beneath the vibration. Waiting for someone to stop long enough to hear it.

Part II

The Theory

Why the Cage Is Inevitable

The Mirror Breaks

The Clinician had worked in healthcare administration for fifteen years when she accepted the management position at the regional medical center's behavioral health clinic. She had her Master's degree in Social Work, her clinical license, and fifteen years of experience. She knew what functional leadership looked like. This wasn't it.

Her new environment made that distinction painfully clear. The clinic's dysfunction was not subtle or hidden. It was visible to anyone willing to look directly at it. Yet it was strangely invisible to the people with the authority to correct it.

One senior manager—we'll call her the Administrator—had burned through three staffed teams of therapists in under two years. These were not isolated departures scattered across time: they were total losses, entire groups of clinicians resigning one after another. Each departure carried the same explanation. HR complaints described the same patterns. The staff all spoke to the same experience. Exit interviews named the Administrator.

The consistency of the data left no other reasonable interpretation. The Administrator was failing in her role, and failing in ways that caused real harm to therapists and patients alike.

But the Administrator had seniority. She attended the meetings that signaled status. She spoke in the organization's internal dialect. She had social capital built from years of proximity to leadership, capital that insulated her from consequences in ways that even deteriorating patient outcomes could not penetrate.

When therapists raised concerns, leadership reframed their concerns as resistance, immaturity, or a lack of understanding of "how organizations work." What was obvious to everyone else became—within the cage of their interpersonal alliances and internal narratives—evidence not of managerial failure but of employee weakness.

The Clinician watched a sequence of competent clinicians leave. Morale declined. Referral times increased. The quality of care quietly collapsed. Yet nothing in the structure changed. No reassignment, no corrective action, no recalibration of leadership. The organizational chart remained fixed. The dysfunction continued undisturbed.

And then, in a gesture that appeared like accountability—but would later reveal itself as ritual—senior leadership hired an outside consultant to conduct an independent assessment of the clinic.

The Consultant spent three weeks onsite. He interviewed staff individually and in groups. He reviewed documents, studied workflows, and traced communication lines as he attempted to understand the underlying dynamics. He spoke with the Clinician and, critically, he listened in a way that suggested he was actually trying to understand what was happening, not simply to confirm a narrative preselected for him.

His findings were not surprising to the clinic's personnel. He identified the Administrator's leadership as the central failure point and the organization's tolerance of that failure as the mechanism perpetuating it. He concluded that, unless the Administrator was removed from her position, the cycle would simply keep repeating.

Three days after presenting his preliminary report, the Consultant was terminated. Leadership declared his findings "inconclusive," reaffirmed their trust in the Administrator, and allowed the dysfunction to continue.

When the Clinician recounted this to me, she struggled to make sense of it. They had hired the Consultant to find the problem. He had found it. Why discard him?

The answer lies not in cynicism or conspiracy, but in the quiet and powerful psychology that shapes how people protect themselves from truths they cannot bear. The executives who brought the Consultant in likely believed they wanted an honest review. They likely believed they were open to difficult findings. They likely believed they valued clarity over comfort. But wanting clarity is not the same as being able to withstand it.

For leadership to accept the Consultant's conclusion, they would have needed to acknowledge that they had defended the wrong person for years, dismissed legitimate concerns, contributed to the departure of skilled clinicians, and allowed patient care to suffer under their watch. This was not an abstract miscalculation; it was a concrete and consequential failure.

Few people can internalize such a truth without their defenses activating. And so the mind, doing what it must to preserve coherence, produces an alternate interpretation. It concludes that the Consultant misunderstood the context. He relied too heavily on negative voices. His methods were incomplete. The situation was more complex than he appreciated. All these objections feel reasonable because they shield the self from unbearable recognition. They are not perceived as excuses. They are accepted as insight.

This psychological pattern blends seamlessly with the structural incentives of organizations. The Administrator's tenure, relationships, and political capital would have made her removal disruptive. Admit the truth about the Administrator, and one must reconsider every decision that placed her in this role and kept her there. Acknowledging the Consultant's findings would have destabilized leadership's self-understanding and their network of internal alliances. The Consultant's presence became intolerable not because he was wrong, but because he was correct in a sense the organization could not accommodate.

In this way, the Cage protects itself. Not through malice or scheming, but through a series of individual decisions that each feel locally rational and collectively preserve the system's coherence. One leader questions the Consultant's methodology. Another feels the recommendations lack appreciation for the clinic's constraints. A third worries about the optics of removing a long-tenured manager. Each objection is sincere. Together, they form a structure that repels any external perspective before it can penetrate.

The Consultant made a predictable error. He believed that evidence would be enough. He assumed that leadership could accept what he found. He mistook the commissioning of an investigation for the capacity to hear its results.

A person cannot be reasoned into acknowledging a truth that their psychological defenses will not permit. When the truth threatens both the self-concept of individuals and the structural equilibrium of the institution, the truth is not integrated. The mirror is declared defective, and those who told the truth become, in retrospect, the complainers whose grievances misled whoever held it.

The Clinician eventually resigned. She recognized that the organization was incapable of seeing itself clearly and that this incapacity was not temporary. It was structural. It was psychological. It was intrinsic to how the place functioned. The therapists kept leaving. The dysfunction remained. The Administrator remained. Leadership remained. And the Cage stayed intact.

This pattern is not unique to healthcare. It is present wherever organizations attempt to diagnose their own failures. A company commissions a strategic review, rejects the findings that would require executives to relinquish their preferred narratives, and concludes that the consultants lacked nuance. A university brings in external reviewers to assess a failing department, dismisses their conclusions when they implicate a beloved chair, and proceeds as if nothing had been learned. A technology firm conducts a listening tour after senior engineers depart, only to produce a report on "communication challenges" rather than address the toxic leadership everyone else already understood to be the problem.

The structure is universal. An organization invites the mirror, sees a reflection it cannot accept, and destroys the mirror. It convinces itself that the mirror was flawed.

We are tempted to explain these events morally, but morality is the wrong frame. The more accurate explanation is the convergence of two truths: human psychology resists information that threatens identity, and consequently formal systems cannot validate themselves from within.

Gödel (1931) established the incompleteness of formal systems. Organizations are formal systems. Their procedures, incentives, metrics, and hierarchies generate blind spots that cannot be resolved internally. They require the external perspective. But external perspective is only useful if the people inside the system can psychologically withstand what it reveals.

If you are in leadership and you commission an external review, you must understand what you are asking for. You are not merely requesting data. You are inviting someone to reveal something you may not be prepared to see. If you cannot hold the possibility that the truth may implicate you, disturb your self-understanding, or require you to revise assumptions you have long defended, then you will dismiss the findings and believe you have done so for sound reasons. The Cage protects itself through the genuine beliefs of the people who maintain it.

The arithmetic of dysfunction is straightforward. The Administrator burns through three teams. Leadership protects the Administrator. A consultant identifies the Administrator as the problem. Leadership removes the Consultant. From within the cage, this appears as responsible judgment applied to flawed external advice.

From outside, it is the obvious, predictable consequence of a system that is incapable of confronting its own reflection. Both interpretations feel sincere. Only one corresponds to reality, and the people inside cannot tell the difference. That is not a moral indictment. It is an acknowledgment of structural limitation.

The cage cannot validate itself from within. When the mirror reflects something the cage cannot bear, the mirror is not examined or assessed. It is eliminated.

And somewhere on the periphery of this failing system, another capable therapist updates her résumé, having learned what competent people always learn in such places: an organization that protects its illusions more fiercely than its mission is not a place where you can do good work.

CHAPTER 5

The Geometry of Scale

In 2010, I spent three weeks comparing two enterprise service buses. MuleSoft and its rival—whose name I can no longer remember—matched feature for feature, line for line. Both had the right connectors, adequate performance, reasonable pricing, credible case studies. After demos and technical analysis, architecture reviews and vendor meetings, the decision came down to something close to a coin flip. We went with MuleSoft.

My team adopted it. Our parent company signed an enterprise agreement. Other firms in our network saw the selection and followed. Within a few years, MuleSoft had become something close to an industry standard in our sector. Salesforce eventually bought them for six and a half billion dollars. I cannot remember the name of the runner-up. Neither can anyone else.

Standards erase alternatives through accumulated defensibility rather than superiority. The coin flip in 2010 was legitimate—the options were genuinely equivalent. The coin did not stay on the table. The flip hardened into precedent, the precedent into justification, the justification into safe harbor. A decade later, choosing the alternative would require explanation. Choosing MuleSoft required none.

The lock-in was precedential. One company chose MuleSoft, documented the choice, defended it successfully. Other companies, facing the same decision, saw that precedent and thought: if we choose MuleSoft and it fails, we can point to everyone else; the decision is defensible. If we choose the alternative and it fails, we stand alone; the decision looks reckless. Each selection made the next safer. Safety was the reason, technology was incidental.

At Ten People

At ten people, the coin still lives on the table. Someone looks at two equivalent paths, shrugs, makes the call. The risk is personal and present—if this turns out badly, everyone will know who decided and why. Judgment is allowed to be faster than proof. The person making the judgment will personally experience the consequences. The organization is small enough that context is shared. "I picked this one because it felt right" is sufficient.

Randomization is rational under genuine uncertainty: two equivalent paths mean flipping a coin avoids paralysis, eliminates bias, forces action. At ten people, the explanation is simple. We had to choose, neither was clearly better, so we chose. The team was in the room. They saw the equivalence.

At One Hundred People

By one hundred people, the same decision needs a trail. The change is geometric. Distance dilutes context. The person reviewing the decision in Finance was not in the room where it was made. The director evaluating the outcome six months later does not have the tacit knowledge the original team had. Prudence becomes a memo, a rubric, a set of documented criteria that can be reviewed by someone who was not present.

The right move must look reasonable to a stranger three years later when the only record is what was written down. The coin flip becomes indefensible under these conditions. Explaining to a director who joined after the decision that a six-million-dollar technology choice was made by flipping a coin is technically accurate and organizationally indefensible. So organizations stop using randomization even when randomization would be appropriate—even when the alternatives are fake precision and manufactured justification.

The engineer writes code that will sail through review—defensible code that uses patterns everyone recognizes, code that can be justified by pointing to precedent if something goes wrong. The manager chooses platforms with the thickest documentation and the largest installed base. Technical superiority matters less than social proof. Nobody gets fired for choosing the industry standard.

The director keeps ceremonies and processes even when they have stopped adding value, deviation being harder to explain than delay. "We followed the standard process and it took six months" is defensible. "We skipped the architecture review because we knew it would not add value and shipped in three months" is harder to defend, even if the shipped product works perfectly. The process exists to create the documentation trail that proves prudence. Skipping the process, even when skipping would be the correct move, removes the documentation and thus removes the defense.

Middle management multiplies to analyze options, ensure compliance, document rationale—improving the defensibility over decisions themselves.

At One Thousand People

By one thousand people, the pressure has settled every-where. As records thicken, judgment thins. The brilliant engineer and the mediocre engineer pass through the same approval gates, fill out the same templates, satisfy the same checklists, and emerge with identical documentation.

Excellence is variance—doing something different, something better, something that deviates from the standard. The system smooths variance because variance is risk, risk is exposure, and exposure is what must be minimized when strangers review the decision.

The system selects for the mean, rewards conformity, and treats even beneficial deviation as threat. The selection is mechanical. When judgment must be demonstrable to strangers, the safest judgment is the judgment that looks like everyone else's judgment. The convergence happens whether leadership wants it or not, whether culture resists it or not, whether individuals fight it or not.

The trajectory from ten to one thousand is compression. Coordination at scale requires legibility, legibility requires formalization, formalization requires standards, standards compress variance. The compression is the cost of coordination. You cannot coordinate one thousand people through shared context and eye contact. You must compress reality into documents, metrics, processes. The compression is lossy. What gets lost are the dimensions that do not fit the frame.

The Initial Public Offering Changes Nothing and Everything

After the IPO, strangers gain legal standing. Before the IPO, the company operates under the same geometric pressures—

scale requires formalization, formalization creates frames, frames compress variance. Private companies at five hundred people face the same coordination challenges as public companies at five hundred people. The frames are already there. The metrics are already there. The documentation requirements are already there.

What the IPO changes is enforceability. Limited liability protects shareholders' capital. Fiduciary duty protects their interests. The business judgment rule protects directors from second-guessing, but only if the decision process appears informed and good-faith when examined after the fact by parties who lack the context the decision-makers had. The documentation that was operationally useful becomes legally required. The formalization that enabled coordination becomes the evidence that demonstrates prudence.

The pressure intensifies at IPO. Companies preparing for the offering often report feeling the culture change before the bell rings. They are anticipating the scrutiny they know is coming, internalizing the constraints, becoming legible to the review they will face. The formalization already present for operational reasons becomes binding for legal ones. The compression that scale created, law amplifies.

Why This Is Inevitable

The geometry is unforgiving. You cannot have one thousand direct reports. The span of control literature establishes the limits: five to seven for complex work requiring judgment, perhaps fifteen for routine work with clear procedures. Past those limits, information gets lost, context gets diluted, judgment gets compressed into metrics that can be aggregated up hierarchies.

Each level of hierarchy is a projection. Three-dimensional reality gets projected onto two-dimensional reports.

The projection preserves some relationships while erasing others. You can rotate the projection, recover some of what was lost, but you cannot eliminate the loss. Multiple projections create multiple partial views, each incomplete in different ways.

The manager two levels up sees dashboards. The dashboards are compressions of compressions. The original context—why this decision made sense, what trade-offs were considered, what tacit knowledge informed the judgment—is gone. What remains are the metrics that survived the projection. The manager makes decisions based on what survived. The system optimizes for what is measured. What is measured is what survived the compression. The compression determines what gets optimized.

This is the cost of operating at scale. Small organizations can rely on shared context, direct observation, judgment calls that do not require documentation. Large organizations cannot. They must compress reality into representations that can travel up hierarchies, across departments, through time. The compression enables coordination. The compression also guarantees loss.

The Substrate Is Civilizational

The demand for predictability originates in civilization itself. Societies require stable expectations. You cannot plant crops without reliable seasons. You cannot start a family without stable social institutions. You cannot save for retirement without currency stability. You cannot build a business without contract enforcement. You cannot make multi-year investments of any kind without reasonable confidence that tomorrow will resemble today within tolerable bounds.

The state's fundamental function is ensuring tomorrow resembles today. It exists to make change predictable enough that people can plan around it, can make commitments that span years, can defer gratification in exchange for future benefit. Civilization is a variance suppression machine. Stability at macro scale enables the long-term thinking that builds cathedrals, cures diseases, puts people on the moon.

The pressure propagates downward: into markets, where investors need predictable returns to allocate capital; into boards, where directors need predictable performance to satisfy fiduciary duty; into governance, where executives need predictable metrics to demonstrate control; into reporting cycles, where managers need predictable progress to justify resources. Eventually it reaches product cycles and engineering schedules, where engineers are expected to deliver on timelines derived from cascading variance suppression originating at civilizational scale.

Macro-stability becomes micro-constriction. The stabilizing force essential at civilizational scale—smoothing volatility, suppressing risk, punishing surprise—becomes constraining in contexts where exploration matters more than stability.

Engineering teams working on eighteen-month innovation cycles do not threaten civilizational stability. They inherit its constraints anyway, because the constraints propagate through every layer of the hierarchy, gaining force at each level until arriving at the engineer's desk as a timeline set by a board meeting, responding to guidance commitments, demanded by markets, required by investors who need predictability to function.

The engineer working on discovery has no authority to resist. The demand arrives encoded in timeline, backed by executive authority, justified by appeals to business necessity. The engineer's protest—"this timeline violates technical reality"—is heard as psychological resistance, as perfectionism, as failure to be scrappy. So the engineer adapts: works nights and weekends, cuts corners that should not be cut, accumulates technical debt that will metastasize, ships broken software, absorbs the blame when customers complain. Eventually, the engineer either internalizes the constraint as correct—"maybe fast is more important than right"—or leaves for somewhere the timeline pressure is less severe.

Engineering as Inversion

Engineering is the inverse of civilization's demand. Civilization requires predictability, stability, smooth variance, known outcomes. Engineering involves emergent complexity, interaction effects, unknown unknowns, discovery-driven iteration, learning under uncertainty. Engineering is lumpy, unpredictable, occasionally messy, fundamentally exploratory.

Engineering, properly supported, takes the time it needs to explore the solution space, fail early and invisibly, stabilize only upon discovering truth. This stands in absolute contradiction to the demand that tomorrow look like today. That contradiction cannot be resolved. It can only be managed, absorbed, or denied.

The pressure is geometric. Scale requires coordination, coordination requires predictability, predictability requires compression, compression loses information. What gets lost are precisely the dimensions that make engineering work— the exploration, the uncertainty, the time required to find the right solution rather than the fastest. The system selects for speed over correctness because speed is measurable and correctness is only visible in retrospect.

The First Force

This is the first force of the Cage, the foundational one. Scale creates pressure toward formalization regardless of ownership, governance, or patience of capital. Ten people can flip a coin. One thousand people cannot. The difference is geometry.

You cannot coordinate at scale without compressing reality into representations. The representations are necessarily incomplete. Organizations optimizing for what the representations capture systematically destroy what the representations erase. This is the cost of operating at scale—invisible because what is destroyed is what the representations cannot capture. Prevention, craft, tacit knowledge, long-term thinking—all erased by frames that measure expense, velocity, legibility, short-term results.

The compression is rational from every perspective. The engineer documents to protect against review. The manager chooses the standard platform to protect against failure. The director implements the ceremony to protect against liability. Each choice is defensible. The aggregate is rigidity. The system hardens through accumulated precedent. What was once a coin flip becomes the only choice that does not require explanation.

Scale alone creates compression pressure. Local frames cannot see global truth. What can be demonstrated dominates what matters. Fiduciary duty amplifies and binds the other three. Each force is independent. All press in the same direction. Their convergence is the Cage.

CHAPTER 6

Organizational Incompleteness

Every organization of sufficient size eventually discovers a disturbing pattern. The metrics look healthy while the system degrades. The dashboards stay green while capability erodes. The performance reviews glow while the best people leave. Everyone in the room knows something is wrong, but the instruments say everything is fine.

The instinct is to blame the existing metrics—to add more metrics, more dimensions, more sophisticated templates. This instinct is understandable—and wrong.

The problem runs deeper than metric design. No measurement system, however sophisticated, can fully capture what matters. This is a permanent property of formal systems themselves.

In 1931, Kurt Gödel proved something that shattered the foundations of mathematics. He demonstrated that any sufficiently rich formal system cannot prove all true statements about itself using only its internal rules. There will always be truths that require external perspective to validate, statements that are true but unprovable within the system's own logic. The proof was devastating because it applied to all formal systems.

The connection lies in formalization. Organizations, like formal systems in mathematics, coordinate through metrics, procedures, documentation, approval processes, governance frameworks. These enable scale. They also guarantee incompleteness.

The Frame

A frame is the collection of metrics, procedures, and documentation that allows an organization to operate. The profit-and-loss statement compresses all economic activity into revenue and cost. The performance review template reduces a year of work into ratings and accomplishments. The incident post-mortem format turns a complex socio-technical failure into root cause and remediation steps. The organizational chart represents reporting relationships as a tree when the actual influence network is a dense graph. The strategic framework collapses uncertainty and optionality into objectives and key results.

Frames are indispensable. A thousand people cannot align on intuition. A board cannot govern on feel. Investors cannot allocate capital based on stories that lack numbers. So organizations create standardized ways of representing reality that allow distributed decision-making, that enable comparison across units and time, that compress high-dimensional complexity into representations that fit on a slide or in a spreadsheet.

Every frame is a projection. It collapses high-dimensional reality into low-dimensional representation through a process that is necessarily lossy. A three-dimensional object projected onto a two-dimensional plane loses depth.

The projection preserves some relationships—relative position, outline—while erasing others—volume, the distance between front and back. You can rotate the object and project again from a different angle, recovering some of what was lost while losing what the previous projection preserved. No single projection captures everything. The reduction from three dimensions to two guarantees loss.

Organizational frames operate the same way. The profit and loss statement projects economic activity onto the revenue-cost plane. It keeps transactions, direct attribution, clean categories. It erases prevention, multiplicative value, option value, hidden dependencies. The performance review projects work onto the accomplishment-impact plane. It keeps discrete achievements, visible initiatives, attributable outcomes. It erases craft, prevention, care work, the gradual accumulation of expertise.

The projection carries implicit values. What the frame keeps depends on what the people who designed it thought the organization should optimize for. What the frame discards becomes invisible—the frame has no dimension to represent it. The Janitor's knowledge of the building does not project onto any axis in the performance review template. From the perspective of someone navigating by that template, the knowledge does not exist.

The Theorem

Any sufficiently complex organization relying primarily on formal procedures, metrics, and documentation to coordinate will systematically undervalue critical work—work that prevents problems rather than solving them, that excels through context-specific judgment rather than codified rules, and that produces value which does not project cleanly into the measurement frame.

This is a claim about what formal systems can and cannot represent. The claim is falsifiable: if you can design a formal system that captures prevention as effectively as it captures remediation, or represents tacit judgment as legibly as it represents documented process, or values diffuse multiplicative contributions as clearly as it values discrete additive contributions, then the theorem is wrong.

You cannot design such a system. The properties being sought contradict each other. A formal system cannot capture the informal. A documentation-coordinated system cannot represent the tacit. A discrete-measurement system cannot value the continuous. Frames can be improved, can be made more sophisticated, can incorporate more dimensions. They remain frames, and frames are projections, and projections lose information.

The loss follows a pattern. Frames preserve what fits their logic and erase what does not. Organizations make decisions based on what the frame shows—when allocating resources, evaluating performance, setting strategy—so they systematically favor work that projects well over work that does not. The frame cannot represent prevention and craft, so the organization navigating by the frame behaves as if they do not exist.

The Gödel Spike

Organizations share the relevant mathematical properties with formal systems. They are rich—they contain enough complexity to make interesting claims about themselves. They are rule-governed—they operate through procedures, metrics, and documentation rather than pure improvisation. They are internally consistent—the rules are designed to cohere, to avoid contradictions, to support each other. And they must make claims about themselves—about their performance, their quality, their soundness, their strategic position.

The Janitor who knows the building is a Gödelian truth (Gödel 1931). The knowledge is real, valuable, observable by anyone who works closely with him. The system has no way to measure "knows the building" in a way that survives aggregation up the hierarchy. The knowledge is too contextual, too tacit, too continuous. It does not decompose into discrete accomplishments that can be listed in a performance review. It does not produce metrics that can be rolled up into dashboards. It does not generate artifacts that can be shown to senior leadership.

So the performance system treats such knowledge as if it does not exist. The system's representational capacity does not include a dimension for this type of knowledge. The frame has no coordinate for "learned the building's rhythms over fifteen years." When the Janitor retires and the building's operations degrade, the degradation is diffuse enough that it does not trigger the alarms that the frame monitors. Coffee quality declines gradually. Restroom supplies run out unpredictably. Conference room mess accumulates slightly longer. Each effect is small enough to tolerate, all together large enough to matter, but none attributable to a single cause the frame can represent.

The recognition arrives suddenly: incompleteness is a permanent property to navigate, not a problem to solve. Call this discontinuity the spike—the moment a system encounters a truth it cannot reach from within. You cannot fix this by adding more metrics. More metrics add more projections, more dimensions, more ways to slice the data. They do not eliminate the fundamental gap between the map and the territory.

Why Metrics Multiply

The natural response to discovering that current metrics miss something important is to add new metrics. Revenue and cost miss prevention, so add uptime metrics. Uptime metrics miss gradual degradation, so add performance percentiles. Performance percentiles miss user experience, so add satisfaction scores. Satisfaction scores miss retention, so add cohort analysis. Each addition is individually justified, each captures something the previous metrics missed, so each feels like progress.

Multiplication of metrics does not eliminate incompleteness. It redistributes it. More dimensions means more projections, and each projection still loses information. The uptime metric captures whether the system is up but not why it stayed up—whether through careful prevention or through lucky absence of stress. The satisfaction score captures whether users report being satisfied but not whether they are learning to work around problems. The retention metric captures whether users stay but not whether they stay because the product is good or because switching costs are high.

Multiplication creates new problems. More metrics means more overhead to collect them, more cognitive load to interpret them, more ceremony to review them. Teams start optimizing for the metrics rather than for the underlying reality the metrics were meant to represent. The metrics become targets, and as Goodhart (1975) observed, when a measure becomes a target, it ceases to be good. The uptime metric gets gamed by defining incidents narrowly. The satisfaction score gets gamed by surveying only happy users. The retention metric gets gamed by making it hard to leave.

Because the metrics are numerous and sometimes contradictory, they enable motivated reasoning. The leader who wants to believe their organization is healthy can always find some metric that supports that belief. Revenue is down but engagement is up. Engagement is down but efficiency is up. Efficiency is down but quality is up. With enough metrics, you can always construct a narrative of success by selectively emphasizing the ones that tell the story you want to tell.

The answer is recognizing that metrics are projections, that projections are incomplete, and that incompleteness is permanent. Once you accept that, you can use metrics appropriately—as partial views that inform judgment rather than as complete representations that replace judgment.

The Prevention Paradox Formalized

Prevention is illegible to formal measurement systems for a reason that goes deeper than poor metric design. Prevention's value manifests as the absence of undesirable events. The site reliability engineer who prevents the outage produces no incident post-mortem, no emergency response, no dramatic recovery story. The security engineer who prevents the breach produces no incident report, no forensic analysis, no remediation plan. The architect who prevents the scaling crisis produces no emergency re-architecture, no heroic all-hands effort, no war room lore.

Absence cannot be measured directly. You cannot count the incidents that did not happen, cannot enumerate the breaches that were prevented, cannot quantify the crises that were avoided. What you can measure are proxies— uptime, vulnerability scan results, load test performance. The proxies are imperfect. High uptime might result from excellent prevention or from lucky absence of load. Clean vulnerability scans might result from good security architecture or from attackers not yet having tried. Passing load

79

tests might result from careful capacity planning or from the test not accurately modeling real traffic patterns.

The imperfection creates ambiguity, ambiguity creates interpretive freedom, interpretive freedom creates political risk. When the platform team asks for more headcount to improve reliability, the CFO asks: how reliable do we need to be? We are already at ninety-nine point nine percent uptime. Is the delta between ninety-nine point nine and ninety-nine point ninety-nine worth the cost?

The platform team cannot prove that delta is worth it because they cannot show the incidents that an even higher reliability would prevent. They can only show probabilities, scenarios, risk models—all contestable, all dependent on assumptions, none with the certainty of actual observed incidents.

So the headcount request is denied. In the absence of clear evidence, the default is no. Prevention can never produce clear evidence because clear evidence would require the counterfactual—what would have happened without the investment—and counterfactuals cannot be observed.

The response team, by contrast, produces clear evidence. When the outage happens, when the breach occurs, when the scaling crisis hits, the response generates artifacts everywhere. Incident reports, post-mortems, remediation plans, executive briefings. The response is legible, attributable, dramatic. The people who responded get recognized, promoted, celebrated. Response is usually less valuable than prevention, but response fits the frame and prevention does not.

This is geometric. Prevention is about what did not happen. Formal systems can only measure what did happen. The gap between those two is the incompleteness. Organizations navigating by formal systems will systematically underinvest in prevention because the formal systems that enable them to coordinate at scale cannot represent prevention's value.

When Frames Become Reality

There is a phase transition that occurs in organizations as they grow. Early, when the organization is small enough that everyone can observe the work directly, the frames are understood as tools—useful simplifications that help coordinate but are not conflated with reality itself.

People know the org chart does not capture actual influence. They know the sprint velocity does not capture actual progress. They know the performance rating does not capture actual contribution. The frames are maps, and everyone remembers they are maps.

As the organization grows and layers of management are added, fewer people can observe the work directly. More people depend entirely on the frames—on reports, dashboards, metrics, templates. For these people, the frames are reality. The metric is the thing. Revenue is value creation. Velocity is progress. The performance rating is the contribution.

When frames become reality, the organization stops optimizing for actual outcomes and starts optimizing for frame-legible outcomes. Teams stop trying to ship good software and start trying to hit velocity targets. Leaders stop trying to build great organizations and start trying to hit quarterly numbers. Individuals stop trying to do excellent work and start trying to get excellent performance ratings.

The optimization is rational from each actor's perspective—the frames determine rewards, so optimizing for the frames is optimizing for success. The collective result is an organization that excels at metrics while degrading at the underlying reality the metrics were meant to represent.

The platform team with perfect uptime gets defunded because they have no incidents to point to, no dramatic stories, no clear ROI. The prevention-focused security team gets deprioritized because they cannot show breaches they prevented. The careful architect who designed systems that scale gracefully gets passed over for promotion because they never had to lead an emergency re-architecture.

Meanwhile, the teams that let things break and then fix them dramatically, that accumulate technical debt and then heroically pay it down, that create crises and then resolve them—these teams get rewarded, because crisis and resolution fit the frame while prevention and stability do not.

This is the inevitable result of navigating by incomplete maps while forgetting they are incomplete. The frames were created to help. They do help—they enable coordination at scale that would otherwise be impossible. They also systematically erase essential capabilities, and when the organization forgets that the erasure is happening, those capabilities atrophy until they disappear.

The Incompleteness Is Permanent

The temptation, upon realizing that organizational frames are incomplete, is to try to complete them. Design better metrics that capture prevention. Create evaluation systems that recognize craft. Build frameworks that represent tacit knowledge. These efforts can improve frames, can make them more sophisticated, can help them capture more of what matters. They cannot complete the frames. The incompleteness is a permanent feature.

This is Gödel's (1931) insight applied to organizations. Any system rich enough to be interesting, consistent enough to be useful, and formal enough to coordinate at scale will have truths it cannot prove, values it cannot measure, knowledge it cannot represent. You can expand the system, add axioms, introduce new dimensions. The expanded system will have its own incompleteness, its own blind spots, its own truths that cannot be validated from within.

The practical implication is that organizations cannot solve the incompleteness problem by building better frameworks. They can only manage it by acknowledging it exists, by documenting what their frameworks miss, by protecting the capabilities their metrics cannot capture, by preserving judgment in domains where formalization would destroy value.

Mode B does this. It operates with multiple frames simultaneously, acknowledges what each frame captures and what it erases, makes the incompleteness itself visible so it can be managed rather than ignored.

Mode A tries to complete the frames, to make metrics comprehensive, to reduce all judgment to procedure. The attempt fails, but the failure is invisible from inside Mode A because Mode A has convinced itself the frames are complete. So Mode A keeps optimizing for what it can measure, rewarding what it can see, defunding what its metrics cannot capture—and capability degrades even as dashboards improve.

Incompleteness explains why frames have blind spots. It does not explain why organizations double down on frames even when the blind spots become visible. Why do competent people, watching the system degrade while the dashboard says everything is fine, keep watching the dashboard? Why do leaders who know that the metrics miss prevention continue defunding prevention? Why does the map win even when everyone can see it is lying?

Scale demands compression. Incompleteness guarantees that compression loses essential information. Two forces remain, and their convergence is what makes the Cage inescapable.

CHAPTER 7

The Forces Converge

Scale demands compression. Incompleteness guarantees blind spots. These two forces alone create pressure
toward formalization—toward metrics, procedures, documentation that enable coordination, while erasing what
cannot be compressed. But the two forces do not explain
why the pressure becomes inescapable, why reforms repeatedly fail, why organizations systematically destroy what
their frames cannot capture even when leaders can see it
happening.

The answer is convergence. Four independent forces,
each arising from different necessities, all pressing in the
same direction.

Four Forces

Scale is geometric. You cannot coordinate one thousand
people through shared context and direct observation.
Reality must be compressed into representations that can
travel up hierarchies, across departments, through time.

The compression is lossy by mathematical necessity. What does not fit the frame gets erased.

Incompleteness is mathematical. Any formal system rich enough to be useful cannot prove all true statements about itself using only its internal rules, Gödel (1931) proved. Organizational frames—metrics, procedures, templates that enable coordination—share this property. They preserve what fits their logic and erase what does not. The Janitor's knowledge of the building, the platform team's multiplicative value, the prevention work that manifests as an absence of failures—all invisible to frames that have no dimension to represent them.

Legibility is epistemic. Formal systems can only operate on what they can represent. Distributed decision-making requires common representations. The representations favor work that can be demonstrated over work that cannot. Prevention that manifests as absence loses to response that generates artifacts. Craft developed over years loses to documented procedure that can be taught in weeks. Local optimization that fits specific context loses to standard practice that can be compared across contexts. What cannot be shown cannot be rewarded. What cannot be rewarded exits.

Law is binding. Corporate law, through fiduciary duty and the business judgment rule, requires that decisions be demonstrably sound when reviewed after the fact by parties who lack the context in which the decisions were made. This transforms operational pressures into legal requirements. The documentation that was once useful becomes mandatory. The formalization that enabled coordination becomes evidence of prudence. The metrics that made distributed decisions possible become justification that can survive judicial scrutiny.

Independence and Alignment

Each force operates through different mechanisms. Scale: information processing limits. Incompleteness: formal system properties. Legibility: representation constraints. Law: accountability requirements. None requires the others to exist. A small organization faces legibility pressure without facing scale pressure. A private company faces scale and incompleteness without facing the legal pressure public companies face.

The forces are independent in origin but aligned in effect. When an organization creates standardized metrics, those metrics enable coordination at scale, provide common language for comparing across contexts, make work visible to distant observers, and generate documentation that demonstrates prudence. Formalization serves all four needs simultaneously.

This alignment is why formalization is so attractive despite its costs. It solves coordination problems, aggregation problems, visibility problems, and liability problems, all at once. The cost—the compression, the information loss, the systematic erasure of essential capabilities—is diffuse and deferred, while the benefits are immediate and concentrated.

Why Convergence Eliminates Escape

A single force can be navigated around. An organization facing only scale pressure could invest in maintaining rich context despite size. An organization facing only incompleteness could document what frames miss and protect those capabilities. An organization facing only legibility pressure could reward invisible work through parallel recognition systems. An organization facing only legal pressure could accept some risk in exchange for operational flexibility.

Convergence eliminates the navigation space. Scale demands formalization for coordination's sake. Incompleteness guarantees formalization has blind spots. Legibility makes what fits frames visible, while erasing what does not. Law makes all three legally binding. Every direction leads to formalization. Every attempt to preserve what formalization erases must itself be formalized to satisfy one of the four forces, creating new blind spots.

You cannot eliminate scale—growth demands coordination. You cannot eliminate incompleteness—formal systems have this property mathematically. You cannot eliminate legibility—distributed decision-making requires common representations. You cannot eliminate law—fiduciary duty is not optional for organizations with external stakeholders. The forces arise from necessities, not choices.

The convergence explains why reforms repeatedly fail. Skunkworks are created to escape scale pressure, but their work must eventually be evaluated using organizational metrics, and that reintroduces incompleteness and legibility pressures. Red teams are established to provide external perspective on blind spots, but their recommendations must be justified through demonstrable process, which reintroduces legal pressure. Consultants are hired to see what internal frames miss, but their findings must be aggregated into decision frameworks that operate under all four forces. Each reform addresses one force, while remaining subject to the other three.

The convergence explains why the problem intensifies with organizational maturity. Young organizations face scale pressure lightly, incompleteness partially, legibility moderately, legal pressure minimally. As the organization grows, goes public, adds stakeholders, increases regulatory scrutiny, all four pressures intensify simultaneously. The forces that were manageable individually become binding collectively.

The Response Choice

Organizations face a choice in how they respond to convergence. The choice is rarely explicit, rarely articulated, rarely understood as a choice at all. But it determines everything.

Mode A: Completing the Frames

Mode A treats frames as complete (or completable). When dashboards show health while capability erodes, Mode A adds more metrics. When performance reviews miss craft, Mode A makes templates more sophisticated. When prevention goes unrewarded, Mode A creates new categories and measures to capture them.

The instinct makes sense. If the current measurement is incomplete, complete the measurement. The leader adds a "prevention" category to the performance review template. HR creates a "craft excellence" award. The CFO commissions a "total value" metric that attempts to capture multiplicative contribution. Each addition is individually justified. Each fails to capture what it names because the properties being measured resist formalization.

Mode A tries to complete the frames, to make metrics comprehensive, to reduce all judgment to procedure. The attempt fails because incompleteness is permanent. But the failure is invisible from inside Mode A because Mode A has convinced itself the frames are complete or nearly complete. So Mode A keeps optimizing for what it can measure, keeps rewarding what it can see, keeps defunding what its metrics cannot capture.

Capability degrades even as dashboards improve. The best people leave while performance reviews glow. Systems break while monitoring shows everything was green. The platform team with perfect uptime gets defunded because they have no incidents to point to. The prevention-focused security team gets deprioritized because they cannot show breaches they prevented. The careful architect who designed systems that scale gracefully gets passed over for promotion because they never had to lead an emergency re-architecture.

Mode A is the default. It is what organizations do when they discover incompleteness and try to solve it rather than navigate it.

Mode B: Navigating Incompleteness

Mode B treats frames as incomplete. It operates with multiple frames simultaneously, acknowledges what each frame captures and what it erases. It makes the incompleteness itself visible so it can be managed rather than ignored.

Mode B does not try to complete the frames. It documents what the frames miss. It protects capabilities the metrics cannot capture. It preserves judgment in domains where formalization would destroy value. It builds parallel systems—the legible ones that satisfy scale, legibility, and law, and the illegible ones that preserve prevention, craft, tacit knowledge, and judgment.

Mode B is rare. It requires accepting that no measurement system, however sophisticated, can fully capture what matters. It requires maintaining capabilities the formal systems cannot see, protecting work the dashboards cannot display, rewarding contributions the performance reviews cannot measure.

Mode B organizations separate external and internal frames. The 10-K filing, the board deck, the performance review template—these must be legally defensible, must use standard language, must minimize variance. They satisfy the convergent pressures. But internal strategy documents can use distinctive language, can explore ideas that would never survive external review, can maintain the variance that external frames must compress.

The separation is explicit and maintained in Mode B. Public language serves legal and coordination requirements. Internal language serves strategic thinking and capability preservation.

Mode B is more expensive. It requires maintaining multiple systems, preserving capabilities that formal frames cannot see, accepting variance that formal systems want to smooth. Mode B is harder to explain—it looks like redundancy, looks like refusal to standardize, looks like attachment to informal practices. Mode B requires leadership capable of operating in multiple frames simultaneously and explaining to boards, regulators, and investors why the organization maintains capabilities that metrics cannot capture.

Mode B is harder still because it must satisfy all four forces for the visible systems, while protecting through invisible systems what those forces erase. The visible systems must coordinate at scale, must aggregate across contexts, must make work demonstrable, must satisfy legal requirements. The invisible systems must preserve prevention, craft, local optimization, and judgment. Both systems must coexist. Neither can be eliminated without losing essential capabilities.

Mode B is the only response that acknowledges what convergence actually is. The forces are permanent properties of operating at scale under formal constraints with legal obligations. They can be managed. They cannot be eliminated.

The Stability Problem

Mode A is the ground state. Left alone, organizations drift there. The four forces—scale, incompleteness, legibility, law—all push in the same direction. Resisting them requires energy.

Mode B is not an alternative equilibrium. It is a deviation from equilibrium, maintained only while some forcing function supplies the energy to hold the system away from its natural state. The forcing functions are few: founder authority backed by voting control, charismatic leadership enforcing uncomfortable norms, private ownership that can ignore external pressure, or some existential threat that shapes variance into survival rather than risk.

When the forcing function weakens—when the founder dies or steps back, when voting control dilutes, when the threat passes, when enforcement of uncomfortable norms relaxes—the system does not stay in Mode B. It drifts back toward Mode A. The reversion is not failure of will or culture. It is the physics of the constraints reasserting themselves.

Apple under Jobs maintained Mode B through personal authority that made board challenge costly. When Jobs died, the forcing function was removed. The drift toward Mode A—schedule over readiness, guidance over product truth—was not Tim Cook's failure. It was gravity. Bridgewater under Dalio maintained Mode B through radical transparency norms that inverted normal social costs. When Dalio stepped back, the norms softened, because maintaining them required energy that the system no longer supplied. SpaceX maintains Mode B through structural protection—seventy-nine percent voting control plus private ownership—that eliminates the feedback loops other organizations cannot escape. The protection is structural rather than personal, which is why it persists.

The implication is uncomfortable: Mode B is not a steady state available to mature institutions under normal governance. It is a phase transition available only under extraordinary conditions, and the phase transition is reversible. The sane strategy is not "become Mode B forever" but rather: recognize when you temporarily have a forcing function, extract as much irreversible progress as the window allows, and design the inevitable reversion to be as graceful and as late as possible.

The Systematic Patterns

When four independent forces converge on formalization, and formalization has systematic blind spots, and organizations optimize for what formalization captures, predictable patterns should emerge. The patterns should be visible across domains, measurable in organizational artifacts, intensifying with organizational maturity.

A careful observer can see them. The patterns appear in resource allocation decisions—through certain kinds of work being systematically defunded despite being essential. They appear in performance evaluation—with certain kinds of contribution being systematically overlooked despite creating value. They appear in strategic language—with variance compressed, distinctiveness erased, and convergence toward standard formulations. They appear in organizational structure—as certain capabilities get systematically eliminated despite preventing catastrophe.

These patterns are not speculation. They are testable predictions about what happens when formal systems meet scale, incompleteness, legibility, and law.

Law amplifies and binds the other three forces—through specific legal doctrines that make process documentation mandatory, the case law that established demonstrable soundness as the standard, the asymmetries that make visible work defensible while making invisible work risky. Law is what transforms operational pressures into legal obligations.

The convergence is real through measurable linguistic compression. If organizations under legal pressure systematically compress strategic language, the compression should be visible in public filings, should measurably intensify with regulatory exposure, should vary predictably across governance regimes. The prediction is testable. The evidence is clear.

The patterns operate at human scale.

CHAPTER 8

The Legal Amplifier

Scale demands compression. Incompleteness guarantees blind spots. Legibility privileges what can be demonstrated. These three forces create pressure toward formalization even in private companies with patient capital and concentrated ownership. An organization at five hundred people faces coordination challenges whether or not it has external shareholders. Formal systems have structural limitations whether or not directors face regular legal scrutiny. Visible work dominates invisible work whether or not anyone reviews the documentation.

But none of these forces makes the pressure legally binding. Law is the fourth force—the amplifier that transforms operational necessity into legal requirement, converting useful documentation into mandatory evidence, making otherwise manageable pressure inescapable.

The Business Judgment Rule

Delaware corporate law governs most American corporations because most choose to incorporate there (Del. Code Ann. tit. 8, § 101(a)). Among its doctrines is the business judgment rule, which prevents judges from second-guessing business decisions with the benefit of hindsight (Del. Code Ann. tit. 8, § 102(b)(7)). Courts presume that directors acted on an informed basis, in good faith, and in the honest belief that their actions were in the company's best interests. As long as those presumptions hold, the decision is protected even if it turns out badly.

This protection is essential. Without it, every poor outcome would trigger litigation, every downturn would invite shareholder suits, and every risk that failed to pay off would expose directors to personal liability. Directors would become impossibly conservative. As Chancellor Allen wrote in *Gagliardi v. TriFoods International*, 683 A.2d 1049 (Del. Ch. 1996), shareholders want directors to take risks. Shareholders can diversify across hundreds of companies; directors have their careers, reputations, and livelihoods concentrated in one. A director who faces personal liability for failure but gains only a tiny fraction of success will rationally avoid all variance. The rule exists precisely to prevent this paralysis.

But the rule contains a profound asymmetry. It protects process. Outcomes are irrelevant. To invoke its protection, directors must demonstrate—after the fact, to parties who were not present—that they engaged in reasonable deliberation. Demonstration requires evidence. Evidence requires documentation. Documentation requires procedure.

Scale already created the need for documentation to coordinate across distance and time. Law makes that documentation legally required. What was operationally useful becomes evidentially necessary. The compression that scale

96

demanded now serves legal defense. The frames that incompleteness made inevitable become mandatory for liability protection. The visibility that legibility privileged becomes binding under judicial review.

What "informed basis" means in practice: Did the board receive written materials? Did they spend adequate time reviewing them? Did they ask the right questions? Did management provide answers? Was the analysis documented? Were alternatives considered? Were risks identified? Was there a record of deliberation? The inquiry is procedural. The question is whether directors can show, through documents, that they followed a process that looks reasonable to a judge reviewing the record years later.

Van Gorkom's Shadow

The Delaware Supreme Court's decision in *Smith v. Van Gorkom,* 488 A.2d 858 (Del. 1985), established how completely process documentation dominates substantive expertise under the business judgment rule. The case involved Trans Union Corporation and its CEO, Jerome Van Gorkom, who had negotiated a merger at fifty-five dollars per share—a substantial premium over market price. The deal looked good. The price was fair, arguably generous. Shareholders were getting a meaningful return.

The court held the directors personally liable anyway. The price was irrelevant. The directors were liable because the process was indefensible. The board had approved the merger after a two-hour meeting without commissioning a formal valuation, retaining investment bankers, or reviewing written analysis of alternatives. Van Gorkom had presented the deal, the board had discussed it, and they had voted to approve.

Justice McNeilly dissented, arguing that the board had 116 years of collective employment at Trans Union and sixty-eight years of combined director experience. He wrote that "directors of this caliber are not folks ordinarily taken in by a fast shuffle." He argued for substantive qualification—the board knew the company, knew the industry, recognized a good deal when they saw one.

The majority rejected this entirely. Expertise could not substitute for documentation. Intuition could not replace formal valuation. The premium price could not redeem the abbreviated process. By rejecting McNeilly's argument, the court established that process documentation is the whole of the business judgment rule in duty-of-care cases. Expertise without paperwork is legally irrelevant.

This is where context dependence meets legal amplification. The board's deep knowledge of Trans Union, their collective judgment about fair value—all the tacit expertise that made their decision sound—was invisible to the court reviewing documents years later. Context that was rich and real to the decision-makers became illegible to the legal system evaluating the decision.

Law privileges what can be demonstrated over what was known. Knowledge that exists in context but cannot be documented becomes, from a legal perspective, knowledge that does not exist at all.

The decision shocked corporate America so severely that Delaware amended its statute within a year. Section 102(b)(7) now allows corporations to eliminate director liability for duty-of-care breaches through charter provisions. Nearly every Delaware corporation adopted such a provision.

But the amendment did not reduce the pressure for demonstrable soundness. It intensified it. With monetary liability eliminated for directors who stay within proper process, the process itself became the only thing that matters. The cage was fortified, not dismantled.

The Process Tax

The legal environment does not prohibit risk. A fully informed board can bet the company on a single product, enter a market with ten percent odds of success, or reject a premium acquisition offer to pursue an uncertain strategy. Delaware courts will not second-guess these decisions. In *In re Citigroup Shareholder Derivative Litigation*, 964 A.2d 106 (Del. Ch. 2009), the court explicitly refused to impose liability for business risks taken over a long time that collectively led to billions in losses during the 2008 financial crisis. The directors had taken enormous risks. The risks had failed catastrophically. The court protected them anyway, because the decisions were made through proper process.

The constraint operates on speed rather than magnitude. To make a defensible decision, directors must pay what amounts to a process tax: investment bankers, fairness opinions, legal counsel, board committees, documented deliberations, formal minutes. This bureaucracy takes time and money. It produces paper trails that satisfy legal requirements but slow the organization's ability to act.

Quick judgment calls based on deep business knowledge create exposure. Three months commissioning studies and retaining advisors creates protection. Both might reach the same decision. Only one can defend it in court. This is scale pressure amplified by legal pressure—what was operationally useful becomes legally mandatory.

The documentation that enabled coordination at scale now serves a second master: liability protection. The process exists both to make better decisions and to prove prudence to strangers reviewing records years later.

The Cage operates through procedure. Delaware law does not forbid risk (Del. Code Ann. tit. 8, § 102(b)(7)). It taxes the process of taking it.

The Rationality Boundary

Delaware law provides one substantive limit: the doctrine of corporate waste. In *Brehm v. Eisner*, 746 A.2d 244 (Del. 2000), the court held that "irrationality is the outer limit of the business judgment rule." A decision is unprotected only if it is so one-sided that no rational business person could approve it—the legal equivalent of "not merely wrong but inexplicable." In *Sample v. Morgan*, 914 A.2d 647 (Del. Ch. 2007), the court allowed a waste claim to survive dismissal when executive compensation appeared inexplicable by market standards. The doctrine rarely results in liability, but its existence shapes behavior.

Genuine outliers—compensation packages, strategic bets, resource allocations that deviate dramatically from industry norms—create litigation risk even when they represent sound judgment. Market rate is the safe harbor. Deviation from market rate requires explanation, documentation, defense.

The standard sounds permissive, and it is. Courts almost never find waste. But the doctrine's existence shapes behavior in ways the cases do not capture. Genuine innovation often looks irrational before it succeeds. Investing billions in unproven technology, rejecting profitable business lines to pursue uncertain ones, betting on markets that do not yet exist—these decisions resemble waste when viewed from outside the context that justified them. The documentation that would make them defensible often does not exist, because the insight that drives them is tacit, contextual, illegible—the very qualities that incompleteness erased from formal frames.

Legibility pressure already favored work that could be demonstrated. Waste doctrine amplifies this into legal requirement. The company that follows its competitors can point to the competitors as evidence of rationality. The company that diverges must justify the divergence on its own terms, with its own documentation, against the inference that doing something different is doing something irrational. Market rate becomes the safe harbor. Industry standard becomes the defense. Conformity is operationally easier and legally safer.

So the waste doctrine truncates the distribution of corporate decisions. Directors regress toward the rational mean—toward industry standard practices, proven strategies, decisions that can be justified by reference to what others have done.

The variance compression that legibility began, waste doctrine completes. The outliers that fail become evidence of irrationality. The outliers that succeed are explained away as luck, timing, or factors the directors could not have predicted. The safe space is the middle. The pressure is toward convergence. The result is the compression of strategic variance into defensible mediocrity.

The Disclosure Trap

If the business judgment rule protects process, shareholder voting should cleanse outcomes. In *Corwin v. KKR Financial Holdings*, 125 A.3d 304 (Del. 2015), the Delaware Supreme Court held that a fully informed, uncoerced shareholder vote invokes business judgment review, effectively immunizing the transaction from post-closing damages claims.

Get the shareholders to approve with full information, and the decision is protected. This looks like democracy solving the coordination problem—let the principals vote directly rather than relying on their agents' judgment.

But full information is a trap. In *Tornetta v. Musk*, C.A. No. 2018-0408-KSJM (Del. Ch. Jan. 30, 2024), the court found that Tesla's shareholder ratification of Elon Musk's compensation package was void because the proxy disclosure was materially misleading. The shareholders voted. The vote was overwhelming—seventy-three percent approved. None of it mattered. The disclosure had failed to reveal the extent of the board's conflicts and the process's defects. A flawed mirror reflects nothing useful. The vote was declared invalid.

This is legibility meeting law at its most brutal. The formal system requires information. The information must be complete and accurate. But completeness is impossible—incompleteness guarantees that some truths about board dynamics, contextual factors, and tacit understandings—however material— cannot be compressed into proxy statements. And accuracy is contestable—what will count as "material" is determined after the fact by courts reviewing the disclosure with adversarial scrutiny.

The response is defensive disclosure—burying shareholders in information to avoid omission claims. Providing every risk factor that might be relevant, every conflict that might be alleged, every alternative that might have been considered. The proxy becomes a document designed for inoculation rather than communication. Shareholders receive hundreds of pages that technically contain all material facts and practically communicate nothing. The frame becomes so comprehensive it ceases to function as communication.

The law demands complete disclosure, incompleteness guarantees complete disclosure is impossible, and the result is documents optimized for legal defensibility rather than shareholder understanding. Legibility taken to its extreme produces illegibility.

The Officer Gap

The protections that shield directors do not extend equally to everyone. Section 102(b)(7) exculpates directors from monetary liability for duty of care breaches, but it does not cover officers. In *In re McDonald's Corporation Stockholder Derivative Litigation*, C.A. No. 2021-0324-JTL (Del. Ch. 2023), the Delaware Court of Chancery allowed claims to proceed against officers for oversight failures that would have been dismissed against directors. The legal structure creates an asymmetry: directors are shielded, officers are exposed.

This creates a second-order distortion. The board might approve a risky strategy—safe within its business judgment rule protection, further insulated by the corporate charter. But the CEO, the CFO, the General Counsel face a different calculus. They lack the statutory shield. A derivative suit can reach them personally. The same decision that is protected at the board level is exposed at the executive level.

The result is predictable. Officers become more conservative than directors. The board approves the moonshot; the C-suite quietly kills it in execution. The board endorses the unconventional strategy; management implements the conventional version. The gap between board authorization and operational reality widens, and engineers wonder why the bold strategy announced in the all-hands meeting becomes the timid initiative that actually ships.

The officer gap explains why innovative companies led by visionary boards still ship conservative products. Directors protected by statute can afford boldness. Officers exposed to personal liability cannot. The gap is architectural, embedded in the legal structure. The boldness dies in translation from board room to operating reality because the people doing the translation face different legal exposure.

The Jurisdictional War

Some are leaving. After the *Tornetta* decision invalidated his compensation package, Elon Musk moved Tesla's incorporation from Delaware to Texas. TripAdvisor moved to Nevada. The trend has a name among corporate lawyers: DExit—Delaware exit.

Nevada and Texas offer a different bargain. Nevada's *Chur* decision, 520 P.3d 310 (Nev. 2022), held that gross negligence does not establish director liability—the standard that trapped the Van Gorkom directors does not apply. Texas Senate Bill 29 codified the business judgment rule with strong statutory presumptions that directors are informed and that their decisions are protected (Tex. Bus. Orgs. Code § 21.419). Both jurisdictions have effectively eliminated the procedural tripwires that plaintiffs use to sustain litigation in Delaware.

The result is a differently located cage. In Delaware, the cage constrains directors through process requirements, while giving shareholders litigation access. In Nevada and Texas, the cage constrains shareholders through pleading standards and liability limitations, while giving directors operational freedom. Controllers who want protection from shareholder suits move to Nevada and Texas. Companies that want the credibility of Delaware's judiciary and its well-developed corporate law stay. The market for corporate law is sorting parties by their revealed preference for different versions of the cage.

But the fact that companies are fleeing at all proves the pressure is real and binding. These are not symbolic moves. Reincorporation is expensive, time-consuming, and signals to markets that the company finds the legal environment constraining enough to justify the disruption.

The Cage is real enough that billion-dollar companies with sophisticated counsel are restructuring their legal domicile to escape it. The exodus validates the theory.

Law is more than one pressure among many. Law is the force that makes the other pressures legally inescapable.

The Amplification Mechanism

The legal environment transforms organizational pressures from manageable properties into binding requirements. Scale creates documentation needs. Law makes documentation mandatory. Context makes local knowledge hard to transfer. Law makes hard-to-transfer knowledge legally irrelevant. Legibility privileges visible work. Law makes invisible work indefensible.

Frames already had blind spots from incompleteness. Leaders could navigate those blind spots through judgment, through tacit knowledge, through contextual understanding that did not fit into templates. Law creates a choice: rely on judgment and accept exposure, or rely on process and gain protection.

The payoff matrix is asymmetric. Judgment that proves right earns no special credit—the outcome would have been the same with more process, and in retrospect the process looks unnecessary. Judgment that proves wrong invites litigation, personal liability, career destruction—the absence of documented process becomes evidence of negligence. Process that proves right earns the same credit judgment would have provided—good outcome, responsible governance. Process that proves wrong is protected by the business judgment rule—the directors followed reasonable procedure; the outcome was unfortunate though not actionable; the failure was not due to breach of duty.

Rational directors choose process. Process does not necessarily produce better decisions—it often does not—but the downside of undocumented judgment is catastrophic, while the downside of documented process is manageable. This is legal amplification in its purest form: taking operational pressures that could be balanced against other concerns and making them legally mandatory.

What was useful becomes required. What enabled coordination becomes evidence of prudence. What scale demanded becomes what law requires for defense.

The choice propagates downward. The board demands documented analysis from executives. Executives demand documented justification from directors. Directors demand documented compliance from managers. Managers demand documented procedure from individual contributors. At each level, the requirement shifts from "be right" to "be defensible." Defensibility requires documentation. Documentation requires process. Process is exactly what formal frames provide. And formal frames, as we have seen, are systematically incomplete—they capture what can be compressed and erase what cannot.

Over time, demonstrable processes proliferate, while undocumentable ones atrophy. The organization learns to optimize for what can be shown rather than for what works. The architect's judgment about technical debt, the operator's feel for when the system is drifting toward failure, the engineer's sense of which warnings matter and which are noise—all erode because they cannot be documented. What cannot be documented cannot be defended, and what cannot be defended gets selected against. This is adaptation to a legal environment that punishes undocumented judgment more severely than it punishes documented failure.

Why This Kills Craft

Craft is undocumentable. You cannot write down how to know when the system needs attention, how to feel when a design is almost right, how to sense when the architecture is accumulating debt that will come due. These are judgments developed through years of practice, refined through feedback loops too subtle to capture in process documents. The knowledge is real, valuable, and observable by anyone who works closely with the person who has it. The formal systems have no way to measure it.

Incompleteness already made craft invisible to formal systems—the frames could not capture tacit knowledge, could not represent judgment developed through experience, could not compress years of pattern recognition into metrics captured on dashboards. Law makes undocumentable craft indefensible craft.

When the reliability engineer leaves and incidents increase, there is no trail showing that her judgment was preventing failures. When the architect departs and technical debt compounds into crisis, there is no record demonstrating that his decisions were holding the system together. From a legal perspective, these capabilities did not exist until their absence caused catastrophe—and even then, the causation is too diffuse to trace clearly.

The organization optimizes for what can be defended: documented processes, measurable outputs, standardized procedures. The platform team adds monitoring dashboards and automated alerts—both defensible because they generate artifacts, neither replacing the architect's judgment about which warnings matter and which are noise. The operations team implements runbooks and escalation procedures—both documentable because they create audit trails, neither capturing the operator's sense of when the system is healthy versus when it is merely passing its checks. Each addition is individually reasonable. Each addresses a gap that became visible when undocumented knowledge disappeared. Each erodes the space for craft by replacing tacit judgment with formal procedure.

The erosion is gradual, invisible, and irreversible until the capability is gone. The organization does not notice the loss because the loss occurs in dimensions that formal systems cannot represent. The metrics show facilities operating normally—cleaning schedules are being met, work orders are being processed, systems are functioning within parameters. The metrics show the platform performing adequately—uptime targets are being hit; incident response times are acceptable; automation coverage is increasing. But the metrics miss the degradation in capability—the loss of the judgment that prevented problems before they became incidents, the disappearance of the knowledge that made operations smooth rather than merely compliant.

The Prevention Double-Bind

Prevention faces a particularly vicious form of amplification. Legibility already made prevention invisible—it manifests as absence of incidents, and absence cannot be counted. Law makes that invisibility legally fatal. Prevention's value is the counterfactual—what would have happened without the investment. Counterfactuals cannot be observed, cannot be documented, cannot be proven to parties reviewing decisions after the fact.

The platform team asking for headcount to prevent outages cannot show the outages that might have occurred.

They can show probabilities, benchmarks, models, risk assessments. All contestable, all dependent on assumptions, none with the certainty of actual incidents. The board reviewing the request must balance uncertain future benefits against certain present costs. In the absence of clear evidence, the default is no. And clear evidence for prevention cannot exist because prevention only succeeds by making nothing bad happen.

The response team, by contrast, produces clear documentation. When the outage occurs, the response generates incident reports, post-mortems, root cause analyses, remediation plans. The incidents are real, documented, undeniable. Investing in response capacity is defensible because the incidents happened, the response was documented, the remediation was tracked. The business judgment rule protects decisions backed by evidence. Response produces evidence. Prevention produces absence.

Law systematically favors response over prevention. If prevention succeeds, the investment looks unnecessary— we spent money but nothing bad happened, suggesting we could have spent less. If prevention fails and an outage occurs anyway, the investment looks inadequate—we spent money and the outage happened anyway, suggesting we should have spent more or, better still, spent differently. The organization that invests in response and neglects prevention can defend both choices. The organization that invests in prevention faces a double-bind it cannot escape through documentation alone.

This is all four forces operating simultaneously. Scale made prevention invisible in aggregated metrics—the absence of incidents across a thousand-person organization does not trigger dashboards the way incidents do. Incompleteness erased prevention from formal frames— the frames measure response time without capturing the judgment that keeps systems stable. Legibility privileged

109

response's visible artifacts—the incident post-mortem is legible, while the prevented incident is not. Law made the preference for response legally rational—investing in response can be defended with documentation, investing in prevention cannot.

The result is systematic underinvestment in the capabilities that prevent problems and systematic overinvestment in the capabilities that respond to problems after they occur. The organization becomes worse at preventing fires and better at fighting them. This looks like progress in the metrics—response times improve, incident resolution accelerates, remediation becomes more sophisticated. But the system generates more incidents because the prevention capability has atrophied. The Cage optimizes for visible response at the expense of invisible prevention, and law ensures the optimization continues.

The Process Ratchet

The legal amplifier ensures that process compounds. Every new risk discovered, every failure mode encountered, every regulatory requirement imposed generates a new process. Each process is individually justified—it addresses a real gap, prevents a real failure, satisfies a real requirement. Once created, it persists because removing it is indefensible.

Removing a process requires proving it is unnecessary. Proving unnecessary requires showing its absence would not cause harm. Showing absence of harm requires observing the counterfactual—what happens when the process is not there. The observation cannot be made safely. If you remove the process and nothing bad happens, you cannot prove the process was preventing something rather than just consuming resources. The absence of incidents might be due to the process having worked, or might be due to luck, or might be due to other factors. The causation is ambiguous. If you remove the process and something bad happens, you have demonstrated that removing it was wrong. The demonstration is career-ending. The asymmetry ensures processes only accumulate.

Death by a thousand processes. Each individually reasonable. Each addressing a real concern. Each producing documentation that satisfies some stakeholder. Collectively they form a sedimentary layer of procedure that makes the organization slow, rigid, unable to adapt. The startup that shipped features in days becomes the enterprise that needs quarters for the same output. The team that made judgment calls becomes the committee that needs approval chains. The leader who could say "I know this is right" becomes the executive who needs three scenarios and a risk matrix before deciding anything.

Scale created the need for some process—coordination at one thousand people requires more structure than coordination at ten. Incompleteness created gaps the initial process missed—the frames could not capture all relevant factors, so additional controls were added to address blind spots. Legibility made process visible while making its costs invisible—the ceremony appears in org charts and documentation, the slowdown appears nowhere. Law makes the process legally required and its removal legally risky—each process becomes embedded in compliance frameworks, audit requirements, board expectations. The ratchet tightens through four independent forces all pointing in the same direction. The organization cannot remove process without accepting legal risk. The accumulation is irreversible.

The Convergence Complete

The Cage is built by four forces. Scale requires formal systems to coordinate across distance, time, and hierarchy—the compression is geometric necessity. Incompleteness guarantees those systems have blind spots—the gaps are mathematical property. Legibility privileges what those systems can capture—the preference for visible work over invisible work is epistemic constraint. Law amplifies all three by making them legally binding, by transforming operational pressures into legal requirements, by converting useful practices into mandatory evidence.

Each force is necessary. Scale enables organizations to accomplish what individuals cannot. Incompleteness is unavoidable in any formal system rich enough to be useful. Legibility enables distributed decision-making by making work visible to people who cannot directly observe it. Law protects shareholders from reckless directors while giving directors room to take risks. None of these forces is pathological on its own. Each serves legitimate needs. Each addresses real problems.

But their convergence creates a system that destroys the judgment, craft, and adaptation that enable organizations to navigate uncertainty. What was useful for coordination becomes required for liability protection. What enabled scale becomes the demonstration that satisfies legal review. What made complexity manageable becomes the frame that erases what matters most. The result is organizations that excel at demonstrating soundness while degrading at actual capability.

Law is the fourth force. Law does not create the Cage. Law makes the Cage inescapable.

On Portability:
Beyond U.S. Governance

The legal analysis in this chapter draws on Delaware corporate law and U.S. securities regulation. Readers elsewhere may wonder whether the framework travels. It does—though the fourth force takes local form.

Scale, incompleteness, and legibility are universal. Coordination pressure exists wherever organizations grow. Formal systems have structural limitations regardless of jurisdiction. Visible work dominates invisible work wherever distributed decisions require common representations.

Law amplifies differently across contexts. Civil law systems rely on statutory codes rather than judicial precedent, creating different documentation requirements but similar formalization pressure. Family-controlled firms face weaker shareholder litigation risk but stronger pressure from relationship-based governance and succession dynamics. State-owned enterprises answer to political accountability structures that substitute for fiduciary duty while generating their own formalization demands. Regulated industries—banking, healthcare, energy—face sector-specific compliance regimes that function much like securities law.

The translation: identify what plays the role of fiduciary duty in your context. What creates the demand that decisions be demonstrably sound to parties absent when the decision was made? That pressure, whatever its origin, amplifies the other three forces. The Cage takes local shape. The geometry is universal.

CHAPTER 9

The Variance Compression Thesis

The Cage is the convergence of four forces: scale demands compression, incompleteness guarantees blind spots, legibility privileges only that which can be shown, law makes all three binding. If this convergence is real, it should leave a measurable signature in organizational artifacts.

The artifact is language.

The Hypothesis

Language is the shadow of governance. When organizations formalize—when they go from private to public, when they accept fiduciary obligations to external parties, when they become subject to legal scrutiny—their strategic language becomes compressed. The compression is adaptation to legal exposure. Organizations learn which language survives legal challenge and which language creates liability.

Over time, the language that survives proliferates, while the language that creates risk atrophies.

We can test this.

Let's consider two documents from the same company: the S-1 filing submitted before initial public offering, and the 10-K filings submitted in the years after. The S-1 represents the company before full formalization, before quarterly scrutiny, before years of comment letters and enforcement risk. The 10-K represents the company after formalization—after the board, counsel, and regulators have all had time to teach the company what language is safe.

If the Cage is real, their language should compress over time. Vocabulary should narrow. Sentence patterns should standardize. Strategic description should become more repetitive, more generic, and optimized more for defensibility than for discovery.

Pre-formalization, language optimizes for persuasion and vision. Post-formalization, language optimizes for legal defensibility and regulatory compliance.

The Measurement

Let's examine S-1 and 10-K filings across multiple cohorts of companies, measuring two properties that capture compression:

Lexical diversity: the ratio of unique words to total words in strategic sections. High diversity means varied vocabulary, distinctive phrasing, linguistic creativity. Low diversity means repetitive vocabulary, standardized phrasing, linguistic convergence toward templates.

Shannon entropy: the unpredictability of word sequences, measured in bits (Shannon 1948). High entropy means the next word in a sequence is hard to predict from the previous words—the language contains surprise, novelty, information. Low entropy means the next word is predictable—the language follows familiar patterns, established templates, standard formulations.

Both metrics capture different aspects of the same underlying phenomenon: how much information the language conveys beyond mere compliance. Diverse, high-entropy vocabulary suggests an organization still using language to think, to explore, to communicate distinctive vision. Compressed, low-entropy vocabulary suggests an organization using language primarily to satisfy legal and regulatory obligations, where the goal is demonstrable soundness rather than distinctive insight.

The Cohorts

Let's select companies representing different formalization pressures:

Pre-SOX (Sarbanes-Oxley Act of 2002) **Tech Giants** (Amazon in 1997, Google in 2004): companies that went public before Sarbanes-Oxley intensified governance requirements, facing public market pressure without the full post-Enron regime.

High-Liability Amplifiers (Coinbase in 2021, Robinhood in 2021): companies in sectors with intense regulatory scrutiny, where language creates direct legal exposure and every statement that could be construed as promise or guarantee invites enforcement risk.

Founder-Insulated (Meta in 2012, Snap in 2017): companies where founders retain super-voting shares and the traditional governance pressure is partially mitigated by voting control that prevents their removal by activist investors or hostile boards.

Born-Caged (Snowflake in 2020, Okta in 2017): companies that went public into an already formalized environment, hiring governance professionals from day one and building for public company requirements well before going public.

Public exposure alone would produce equal compression across all cohorts. The degree of regulatory intensity predicts that high-liability companies should compress most. Founder control should blunt the effect of external pressure. Born-caged companies should enter already compressed, if learning from existing public company constraints drives adaptation.

The Evidence

Post-IPO, every company shows compression. The degree of compression varies by cohort, exactly as the theory predicts, but the direction is universal.

Lexical diversity measures the ratio of unique words to total words, ranging from 0 (infinite repetition) to 1 (every word unique). Shannon entropy measures bits of surprise per word; human language typically ranges from 3.5 to 5.0 bits, with higher values indicating more information, more variance, more linguistic creativity (Shannon 1948).

The pattern in filings is stark. High-liability companies compress most dramatically. Coinbase's lexical diversity drops from 0.73 to 0.49, entropy falls from 4.97 to 3.87—a compression of roughly a third in vocabulary and more than a full bit in unpredictability. Robinhood shows similar compression: from 0.69 to 0.47 in diversity, from 4.85 to 3.82 in entropy. These companies operate in sectors where every word in a public filing can become evidence in enforcement actions, where strategic language creates litigation risk, where the legal department reviews every sentence for regulatory exposure.

Founder-insulated companies compress significantly less. Meta moves from 0.70 to 0.63 in diversity, from 4.88 to 4.52 in entropy. Snap shows comparable patterns: from 0.72 to 0.65, from 4.93 to 4.58. They still compress—public market pressure is real even with voting control—but their shift is roughly half as severe as in the high-liability examples. Zuckerberg can say things in Meta's filings that a conventional public company CEO would be advised against. The statements create variance, and variance creates scrutiny, and scrutiny creates risk for directors who lack voting control. With voting control, that risk calculus changes.

Born-caged companies enter already compressed and compress only marginally further. Snowflake's diversity shifts from 0.55 to 0.53, entropy from 4.18 to 4.09. Okta: from 0.57 to 0.55 in diversity, from 4.24 to 4.15 in entropy. Their S-1 filings read like mature public company documents because they were drafted by people who had internalized public company constraints. These companies never had a high-diversity, high-entropy phase. They were optimized for legal defensibility from conception.

Pre-SOX tech giants fall between the extremes. Amazon and Google both show substantial compression (diversity dropping roughly from 0.14 to 0.15 points, entropy falling from 0.61 to 0.62 bits) but less dramatically than high-liability companies and more significantly than founder-insulated ones—exactly what the theory predicts for companies facing public market pressure without either extreme regulatory scrutiny or founder protection.

A skeptic might attribute compression to professionalization—specialized legal and Investor Relations teams write the filings, so language standardizes without strategic cognition narrowing. This explanation cannot account for the liability gradient. If professionalization drove compression, similar-sized companies would compress similarly. They do not. High-liability firms compress more dramatically than low-liability firms of comparable scale and maturity. The pressure comes from legal exposure—not from the communications department headcount.

What Compression Reveals

The compression has nothing to do with writing quality, although the 10-K filings are often more polished than the S-1 filings, more professionally edited, more carefully structured. The compression is about reducing variance, eliminating distinctiveness, converging toward standard formulations that have been legally and regulatorily tested.

Amazon's 1997 S-1 describes its mission as: "Our goal is to be Earth's most customer-centric company, where people can find and discover anything they want to buy online." Specific, concrete, distinctive. By the mid-2000s 10-Ks, the mission becomes: "We seek to be Earth's most customer-centric company, offering our customers low prices, convenience, and a wide selection of merchandise." Still Amazon, but the language has standardized—"seek to be" rather than "goal is," "offering" rather than "where people can find," the addition of "low prices, convenience, and a wide selection" because those are defensible value propositions, while "anything they want to buy" invites overpromise arguments.

Google's 2004 S-1 contains the famous "Don't be evil" discussion and declares: "We aspire to make Google an institution that makes the world a better place." By the 2010s, the 10-Ks describe the mission as: "To organize the world's information and make it universally accessible and useful." The shift is from aspirational to operational. Aspirational language creates expectations. Operational language describes services. Expectations can be challenged in litigation. Services can be documented and defended.

Coinbase's compression is the most dramatic. The 2021 S-1 discusses "the future of an open financial system" and "empowering billions of people." Within two years, the 10-Ks focus on "compliant infrastructure for the cryptoeconomy" and "products designed to meet regulatory requirements." The aspiration has not changed—Coinbase still believes in the mission. But the language has been scrubbed of anything that could be used against them in intense regulatory battles. Every statement must be defensible, every claim documented, every vision hedged.

This compression happened while Coinbase was simultaneously fighting the SEC in court, being investigated by multiple state regulators, and facing congressional hearings. Every word in their public filings was potentially evidence in multiple proceedings. The compression was legal survival.

The Waste Doctrine's Shadow

The waste doctrine explains where compression converges.

In *Brehm v. Eisner*, 746 A.2d 244 (Del. 2000), the Delaware Supreme Court held that irrationality marks the outer limit of the business judgment rule—a decision so one-sided no rational business person could approve it. In *Sample v. Morgan*, 914 A.2d 647 (Del. Ch. 2007), the court allowed a waste claim to survive dismissal where executive compensation appeared inexplicable by market standards. Courts almost never find waste. The doctrine rarely produces liability. Its function is subtler: it makes conformity the safest available defense.

A board that approves executive compensation at market rate faces minimal litigation risk—the market itself validates the decision. A board that approves compensation dramatically above market must explain why the deviation was nevertheless rational. If the bet pays off, the explanation is easy. If the bet fails, the deviation looks like waste.

The same logic applies to strategic language. A company that describes its strategy using standard frameworks—growth vectors, competitive moats, market positioning—is using language that has been industry-validated. Thousands of other companies use the same phrases. The language itself becomes evidence of rationality. A company that describes its strategy using distinctive language, novel frameworks, unconventional formulations must defend the distinctiveness. If the strategy succeeds, the language looks visionary. If the strategy fails, the language looks like evidence that the decision makers were thinking outside the bounds of what any rational board would do.

The waste doctrine does not create compression. It determines where the compression flows: toward market-rate pay and market-standard language. Deviation in either requires explanation, and explanation creates exposure, and exposure creates risk that rational directors avoid.

The Mechanism

Compression happens through learning.

Companies file their first 10-K and receive comments from the SEC. The comments are in the public record. Legal counsel reviews them, identifies patterns in what triggers questions, adjusts language in subsequent filings. Investor Relations gets feedback from analysts about which formulations are clear, which create confusion, which generate unwelcome questions on earnings calls. The board's audit committee reviews the language for litigation risk. Outside counsel flags statements that could be construed as forward-looking without proper safe harbor treatment.

Each round of review removes variance. Distinctive phrasing gives way to tested formulations. Specific examples become generic descriptions. Ambitious claims acquire disclaimers and qualifications. Everyone involved is trying to make the document defensible, and defensibility means convergence toward language that has survived scrutiny before.

The same learning happens across companies. Counsel working on multiple filings see which language survives SEC comment and which triggers additional review. Templates emerge. Entire paragraphs migrate from one company's filing to another's because those paragraphs have been battle-tested. The convergence is rational for each company: why take risks with language when proven formulations are available?

The result is an industry that speaks in increasingly standardized language about increasingly standardized topics using increasingly standardized structures. The underlying businesses may be genuinely distinctive. The language describing them must satisfy legal and regulatory constraints that reward standardization and punish outliers.

What This Means for Strategy

When strategic language compresses, strategic thinking tends to follow. It is possible to think distinctively while writing generically, but the grain runs the other way. Language shapes thought. The words available influence what ideas can be clearly formulated. When strategic planning relies on documents, and documents must use compressed language, and compressed language gravitates toward standard formulations, strategic thinking gravitates toward the same grooves.

The planning process becomes: identify the standard strategic frameworks (growth vectors, competitive moats, market position), fill in the template with company-specific details, produce a document that looks like every other strategic plan except for the numbers. The document is defensible—it follows best practices, uses established frameworks, can be shown to the board as evidence of rigorous process. It is unlikely to contain genuinely novel strategic insight because genuinely novel insight does not fit standard templates.

Mode A organizations live here. Their planning processes are optimized for legal defensibility rather than strategic discovery. The business review deck must follow the standard format. The strategy document must use the standard frameworks. The board presentation must make the standard arguments. Variance gets smoothed out in review cycles. Distinctive thinking gets flagged as unclear or risky. Novel approaches get questioned for lack of precedent.

Mode B organizations maintain two registers. External filings—the 10-K, the proxy, the earnings scripts—must be legally defensible, must use standard language, must minimize variance. Internal strategy documents can use distinctive language, can take risks with formulation, can explore ideas that would never survive SEC review. The separation is explicit and maintained intentionally. Everyone understands that public language serves legal requirements, while internal language serves strategic thinking.

The Broader Pattern

Language compression is easiest to observe in filings because filings are public, structured, and comparable. The same dynamic plays out everywhere inside the firm.

Email language compresses as people learn which phrasings survive forwarding to leadership, which get them in trouble, which generate threads they later regret. Meeting language compresses as people learn which arguments land with executives, which are dismissed without examination, which lead to follow-up requests they would rather avoid. Strategy language compresses as people learn which frameworks boards recognize, which they reward, which they treat as suspect.

Each individual adapts. They use more of the language that works—meaning, the language that achieves their goals without creating personal risk. Over time, the organization converges on a shared vocabulary, shared phrases, shared ways of describing problems and solutions. The convergence enables coordination.

It also erases distinctiveness. The linguistic creativity that often signals genuine insight gets sanded down. When everyone is using the same language, everyone is thinking in the same grooves. Problems get formulated in standard ways, solutions get proposed in standard forms, strategic choices get presented as selection among standard options.

The organization becomes linguistically efficient and strategically constrained.

The Signature

Evidence for the variance compression thesis proves that the Cage is real, is measurable, and operates through mechanisms we can trace. The legal environment creates pressure.

Language adapts. Thinking follows language. Strategy compresses.

The signature appears elsewhere. Forced ranking systems. Performance reviews. Resource allocation. Strategic planning. Anywhere organizations use formal systems to evaluate, the same compression manifests.

The Cage Yields

When Desperation Lowers Defenses

The Clinician's healthcare organization rejected external truth. The Consultant identified the toxic manager. Leadership eliminated the Consultant. The organization protected its illusions and lost capability it could not acknowledge was being destroyed.

This is the norm. Organizations reject external perspective until the cost of rejection exceeds the cost of seeing. The question is: what conditions allow organizations to reach that threshold?

Industrial design in the 1970s rested on a particular internal logic. The schools that trained designers taught a narrow interpretation of modernist restraint. The companies that hired them rewarded work that aligned with that doctrine. Students came to understand that deviation would not be dismissed quietly but corrected publicly. Over time, these norms hardened. They stopped being guidelines and became identity. "Good design" ceased to be a matter of judgment and was treated as the natural shape of intelligence itself.

Luigi Colani did not emerge from that lineage. His attention was on aerodynamics and anatomy rather than grids and right angles. His objects were not composed; they appeared to have grown. This alone would have placed him outside the establishment's trust. His commentary about the establishment placed him further still. He was unrestrained in his criticism and unconcerned with the social costs of expressing it. To a discipline built on shared assumptions about taste, coherence, and pedigree, he was not merely incorrect. He was intolerable.

Some institutions reacted openly. Reportedly, a German design school prohibited students from attending his exhibitions and threatened failing grades for anyone who cited him. Long after those decisions ceased to have consequences, graduates continued to reject his work as unserious and indulgent.

This is not unusual. Once a system has invested enough of its identity in its own preferences, evidence that contradicts those preferences is difficult to process. It is not evaluated. It is removed.

Colani was not dependent on the system's approval. He had the financial independence and personal confidence to continue working without institutional support, and this made him even easier to dismiss. It allowed the establishment to treat him as an eccentric rather than as a valid challenge. He could be ignored without consequence so long as the system remained stable.

It did, until it didn't.

Canon, in the early 1980s, faced increasing pressure in the professional camera segment. While their consumer cameras dominated the market, their professional SLR line had grown stagnant against Nikon's prestige offerings. For a company that had once set the pace, following rather than leading felt like decline.

Under these conditions, an institution's defenses weaken. When the familiar methods stop producing results, the logic that excludes outsiders becomes harder to justify.

Canon did something it rarely did: it initiated a genuine collaboration with someone far outside its norms. Colani produced a series of concepts that, in other circumstances, would have been rejected immediately. Instead, the internal team worked with him. The more extravagant elements were tempered by engineering constraints, but the underlying insight was preserved. The resulting camera, the T90, introduced ergonomics and control placement that seemed foreign at the time but would become standard for decades. When it's placed beside cameras produced thirty years later, their lineage is obvious.

What changed was not the truth of Colani's ideas. His understanding of ergonomics was equally valid in 1975 and 1983. What changed was Canon's capacity to receive them. In ordinary times, his perspective was incompatible with the establishment's self-understanding. Under pressure, the cost of exclusion became higher than the cost of consideration. He was not celebrated. His philosophy was not embraced. But his insight was allowed just enough access to become useful.

The Pattern

The difference between the Clinician's healthcare organization and Canon is not that one had better leadership or stronger culture. Both organizations faced external truth that contradicted internal narrative. Both had mechanisms to reject that truth. The difference was the threshold.

The Clinician's organization was dysfunctional but stable. The behavioral health clinic was failing, but the failure was contained. Turnover was high but manageable. Patient outcomes were poor but defensible. The organization could maintain its illusions without facing existential threat. When the Consultant offered a mirror that reflected uncomfortable truth, rejecting the mirror was cheaper than confronting the reflection.

Canon was successful but stagnating. Market position was eroding. Competitors were innovating. Canon's comfortable assumptions about design orthodoxy were failing to produce competitive advantage. The organization was approaching a threshold where maintaining illusions would cost more than confronting them. When Colani offered perspective from outside the frame, the cost of rejection exceeded the cost of consideration.

The difference is structural. Formal systems cannot validate themselves from within. Gödel (1931) proved this for mathematics. Organizations inherit the same limitation. They require external perspective. But external perspective threatens identity, disturbs self-understanding, and demands revision of defended assumptions. Most organizations reject it until desperation makes acceptance less costly than rejection.

The Clinician's organization rejected the Consultant while dysfunction remained containable. Canon accepted Colani's innovation when stagnation made orthodoxy expensive. The threshold is cost.

Most organizations are closer to the clinic's situation than to Canon's. Stable dysfunction is sustainable. Protected illusions can persist for decades. The Mirror requires conditions that most organizations never reach—and some that reach them lack the leadership to tolerate what the Mirror reveals.

The window, when it opens, does not stay open long.

Part III

The Proof

Measuring the Cage's Effects

CHAPTER 10

When the System Fails

Forced ranking terminates the wrong person more than half the time. Every quarter, the email arrives: "Identify the bottom fifteen percent of your team for performance improvement plans." The engineering manager stares at her roster: twelve exceptional engineers, who delivered everything asked of them, who supported each other, who created technology powering half the company's revenue.

She knows her "bottom" three are stronger than most teams' top performers. She knows that if any of them left, the loss would be material, measurable, visible within weeks. But the curve demands its sacrifice.

Convergence—four forces meeting at the point where organizations must evaluate people, producing systematic errors that are mathematically inevitable, structurally biased, and legally entrenched.

The Mechanism

Forced ranking rests on an assumption so intuitive it rarely gets examined: that each team's distribution mirrors the company's distribution. If fifteen percent of the company underperforms, then fifteen percent of each team underperforms. Apply the curve locally, aggregate the results, and you have identified the company's weakest performers.

The assumption is false, and the errors are mathematical rather than cultural.

Consider a simulation. Nine hundred ninety-four engineers distributed across one hundred forty-two teams of seven. Each engineer has a true performance score drawn from a normal distribution—actual capability, objectively real. Teams form randomly. Managers measure perfectly. No bias, no politics, no miscalibration. The only policy is the curve: each team must identify its bottom performer for termination.

Under these idealized conditions—random teams, perfect measurement—thirty-two percent of terminations hit the wrong person (see Appendix A for methodology). One in three. The person terminated from a strong team outperforms the person retained on a weak team. The curve cannot see this because the curve operates locally while performance distributes globally.

Now make one adjustment toward reality: manager quality varies. Good managers recruit better, develop better, retain better. Their teams are not random samples; their teams are selected. Model this with a manager quality score that influences team composition, and run the same simulation.

The error rate rises to fifty-three percent. More than half. The system now performs worse than random selection. You would identify weak performers more accurately by ignoring the rankings entirely and just choosing names from a hat.

The precise numbers depend on assumptions—how much manager quality varies, how strongly it correlates with team composition. Under different parameters, the error rate shifts. Under no realistic parameters does it become acceptable.

The mechanism holds across the range: forced curves applied to heterogeneous populations produce systematic misclassification. The curve assumes homogeneity. Reality carries variance. The gap between assumption and reality is where careers are destroyed.

Force 1: Scale Demands Aggregation

You cannot have 1,000 direct reports. The span-of-control limit is not cultural preference—it is information-processing constraint. Past five to seven reports for complex work, coordination breaks down. So organizations add layers. Each layer requires aggregation. Performance must be compressed from local observation into transportable representation.

The forced ranking mechanism is one solution to this aggregation problem. It creates a common frame: percentile rankings that can be compared across teams, rolled up through hierarchy, and used to make resource allocation decisions at scale. Without some form of aggregation, distributed performance evaluation is impossible.

But aggregation requires assuming that local samples reflect global distribution. A team of seven people must be treated as a miniature of the broader population. This assumption is necessary for the aggregation to work. It is also false. Scale doesn't just demand aggregation—it guarantees the aggregation will be lossy. The compression necessary for coordination at scale ensures that what gets lost is precisely the information needed to evaluate accurately.

Even if every other assumption held—even if all teams had identical means and variances, even if measurement were perfect, even if managers had no biases—the scale problem alone would create errors. Local samples cannot reliably reveal their position within global distributions. This is sampling theory. The forced ranking mechanism pretends otherwise. The errors are inevitable.

Force 2: Context Hides Team Quality

Manager quality varies. Some managers are excellent at recruiting—they attract top performers and assemble strong teams. Some managers are excellent at development—they take mid-level engineers and grow them into senior contributors. Some managers are excellent at retention—people want to work for them, so their best people stay. These differences create team quality variance.

This is Incompleteness at human scale. The formal system has no field for "manager quality" or "team composition"—these truths exist but cannot be represented within the frame. What the frame cannot represent, the frame cannot adjust for.

Team A, managed by someone excellent at all three, has mean performance of seventy. Team B, managed by someone average, has mean performance of fifty. Both teams have seven people. Both face the fifteen percent curve. Both must identify one person for termination.

Team A terminates someone performing at sixty-five. Team B terminates someone performing at forty. The person cut from Team A is stronger than most people retained on Team B. Both teams were formed recently from the same hiring pool. Team A's manager built a stronger team. Forced ranking cannot see that context.

The context is invisible at the level where the curve is applied. The policy assumes all teams have the same mean. The policy has no mechanism to observe or adjust for manager quality, team composition, or the strategic importance of different teams. The assumption of equal means is built into the mechanism. The assumption is false. The errors follow mechanically from that false assumption.

Calibration attempts to solve this by bringing managers together to compare notes. But calibration operates under the same constraints—managers cannot provide objective cross-team comparisons because performance across different contexts cannot be reduced to a single scalar. Calibration becomes political: the manager with more organizational capital, better rhetorical skill, or stronger executive relationships gets better outcomes for their team. The outcome shifts the bias without reducing it.

Context variance—the fact that teams differ in ways formal systems cannot see—never resolves. The specific differences shift; the blindness is structural. Forced ranking pretends otherwise. The errors compound.

Force 3: Legibility Makes Visible Work Dominate

Even within a single team, not all contributions are equally visible. The engineer who prevents the outage produces no artifacts. The dashboards stay green. From the performance system's perspective, nothing happened. The engineer who resolves three outages has incident reports, post-mortems, measurable customer impact. The response work is visible. The prevention work is invisible.

The same asymmetry appears in care work. The engineer who mentors across teams, who documents tribal knowledge, who creates space for junior engineers to learn performs work that is essential but produces no metrics. The engineer who ships features has commits, velocity, visible output. When the manager must rank people for forced calibration, visible work provides ammunition. Invisible work does not.

Self-promotion compounds the bias. Forced ranking requires advocacy. Your manager argues for you against other managers. If you have not equipped your manager with specific achievements and quantifiable impact, you lose the negotiation. Self-promotion is required. Self-promotion is also policed asymmetrically—research shows women face backlash for self-advocacy that men do not face. The system requires behavior it punishes when performed by people who lack social capital.

Contribution appropriation creates another visibility gap. The idea proposed in a meeting gets credited to whoever repeats it most loudly or presents it most visibly. Collaborative work gets attributed to whoever had the most visible role. Over time, some engineers accumulate visible credit for work they did not solely create, while others see their contributions systematically attributed elsewhere.

Legibility—the fact that formal systems can only measure what projects onto their frames—is permanent. Forced ranking operates on what managers can defend in calibration. What can be defended is what is visible. The invisible work, however valuable, provides no ammunition. The errors are systematic, not random.

The Convergence

Four forces converge to make forced ranking catastrophically broken. Scale demands aggregation: teams must be compared using common frames. Incompleteness hides team quality: the common frame assumes equal means when means vary drastically. Legibility privileges visible work: the evidence available for comparison is systematically biased. Law privileges documented process: the broken system is legally safer than judgment-based alternatives that would be more accurate.

Each force alone would create problems. Together, they create error rates over fifty percent. Worse than random selection. The engineer doing prevention work on a strong team is exactly the person most likely to be terminated.

Prevention is invisible (legibility). Strong teams face equal curves despite unequal quality (incompleteness). The comparison must happen through formal frames that cannot capture either dimension (scale). And judgment that could correct these errors is legally riskier than documented process that perpetuates them (law).

This is convergence. The same forces that compressed language in strategic filings now compress careers. The same physics that created the cost-center mirage and the supervisor's dilemma now creates systematic misclassification at human scale.

Why It Persists

If the errors are provable, if the harm is measurable, if the logic is demonstrably false, why do organizations persist in using forced ranking?

Because it produces documentation. The documentation satisfies legal requirements. A manager who terminates someone based on forced ranking can point to the policy, the calibration session, the stack rank. The decision is defensible even when wrong. A manager who refuses to terminate anyone, who claims their entire team is strong—that manager's judgment is harder to defend. It looks like favoritism, like lack of accountability, like failure to manage performance.

From a legal perspective, documented process beats undocumented judgment even when the process produces systematically wrong outcomes. This is the Cage at human scale. The legal requirement for defensibility, combined with the business judgment rule's protection of process over outcomes, selects for systems that generate evidence even when the evidence is built on false assumptions.

Forced ranking survives not because it works, but because it satisfies the demand for demonstrable soundness. The documentation trail protects directors, satisfies audit committees, provides cover when terminations are challenged. HR and legal departments prefer it despite its failures, because the alternative—trusting manager judgment, accepting that some teams might be uniformly strong—creates perceived risk. An "objective" curve feels safer than judgment, even when the curve is objectively wrong.

The comfort is not about accuracy. It is about defensibility. In organizational environments, where legal exposure drives decision-making more than operational effectiveness, defensibility wins. Every major company uses forced curves or some variant. The practice has become industry standard. And in corporate law, following industry standard is itself a form of protection. The business judgment rule looks more favorably on decisions that follow common practice, even when common practice is mathematically broken.

This is why evidence does not change behavior. Showing boards the fifty-three percent error rate does not eliminate forced ranking. Three reasons: First, the system produces documentation that protects from legal liability—even broken systems feel safer than judgment. Second, accepting the proof would mean acknowledging years of harmful decisions, so psychological defenses are triggered that evidence cannot penetrate. Third, following industry standards provides cover—if everyone is using forced curves, adopting them cannot be irrational under the business judgment rule's framework.

The system persists because all four forces reinforce it. Scale, context, and legibility create the measurement errors. Law makes those errors legally preferable to judgment that would be more accurate, but harder to defend.

What This Proves

Forced ranking is not an isolated dysfunction. It is a demonstration of how the Cage operates when all forces converge at human scale. You have seen the forces named. You have seen language compression as organizational artifact. Now you have seen convergence as systematic human cost.

But you have seen the convergence first because convergence is what you feel when you stare at the roster and know that the people you are about to sacrifice are better than most people who will be retained.

The forces are not separate. They compound. And their convergence is measurable, systematic, and inescapable.

The Cage is real. The proof continues.

CHAPTER 11

The Scale Trap

The Engineering Director has forty-seven direct reports. She knows this is insane. Research on span of control has been consistent for decades—five to seven direct reports for complex work, twelve to fifteen for routine. Forty-seven represents a different category of failure. The company grew faster than the organizational structure could adapt. Headcount approvals came through in bursts. Teams got assigned to her because "she could handle it." For six months, she has been trying to get approval to hire managers who would take on some of these teams. The request keeps getting delayed—hiring managers means additional overhead, and Finance is watching the ratio of managers to individual contributors.

So she does what she can. She meets with each team lead weekly. She reviews their updates. She approves their decisions. She tries to maintain awareness of forty-seven people's work, challenges, career trajectories, and interpersonal dynamics. She knows she is failing because the task is information-theoretically impossible.

She cannot hold forty-seven people's contexts in working memory. She cannot observe their work directly. She cannot distinguish between the engineer who is genuinely struggling and the engineer who had a bad week. She cannot see when someone is being underutilized or when someone is burning out. She relies on what the team leads tell her, and the team leads are themselves trying to compress their teams' realities into updates that fit in thirty-minute meetings.

When performance review season arrives, she must evaluate forty-seven people. She does not know most of them well enough to write meaningful assessments. She asks the team leads for input. The team leads provide summaries. She converts the summaries into ratings and review text. The reviews are generic, vague, useless. The strong performers feel unrecognized. The weak performers receive no specific guidance. And she knows that her evaluations are compressions of compressions, so far removed from the actual work that they have almost no relationship to reality.

The Scale Trap is this geometric fact: human beings cannot maintain direct observation past a certain number of people, and every layer added to solve that problem introduces information loss that compounds through the hierarchy. Scale operates irrespective of context that hides team quality differences, legibility that makes visible work dominate, and legal pressure that demands documentation.

The Geometry of Relationships

The span-of-control limit is combinatorics. In 1933, V.A. Graicunas published a mathematical analysis of the relationships a manager must track. The result explains why forty-seven direct reports is categorically impossible.

A manager with three direct reports maintains eighteen relationships. Three direct relationships (manager to each report), six cross-relationships (each report's relationship with each other report, as perceived by the manager), and nine group relationships (the manager with various combinations of reports). The math is not intuitive, which is why organizations routinely underestimate the burden they impose when they widen spans.

With five direct reports, the relationship count reaches one hundred. With ten direct reports, it exceeds five thousand. The function is combinatorial—as the set grows, the number of possible group configurations explodes. A manager cannot track five thousand relationships. The manager can hold perhaps a dozen in active awareness at any moment, cycling through others as attention permits. The rest exist in a fog, updated only when something forces them into view.

This is why research converges on consistent ranges (Miller 1956; Sweller 1988; Tversky and Kahneman 1971). For complex knowledge work requiring judgment and coordination, effective spans cluster between five and seven. For routine work with standardized procedures, spans can reach twelve to fifteen. Beyond fifteen, even for simple work, the relationship load exceeds cognitive capacity. The manager stops managing and starts triaging—responding to whatever is loudest, missing whatever does not demand attention, making decisions with partial information because complete information is no longer accessible.

The Engineering Director with forty-seven reports is not managing poorly. She is not managing at all, in any meaningful sense of the word. She is processing signals, making guesses, and hoping the system holds together despite her inability to see it. The geometry guarantees this outcome. No amount of skill, dedication, or time management can control five thousand relationships that must be tracked with a brain able to hold seven items in working memory.

The Scaling Cliff

Flat organizations work until they don't. The transition is a cliff, and the drop happens between one hundred and three hundred employees, with remarkable consistency.

GitHub operated without managers for years. Engineers self-organized around projects. Coordination happened through shared context and direct communication. The model worked because everyone could hold the whole company in their head—who was building what, how projects connected, where help was needed. In 2014, at three hundred employees, the model collapsed. CEO Chris Wanstrath described the failure: "Before, we all had to share the road maps in our head. I might be building something here, not even knowing that Paul is building something over here. That worked out fine until we got more people and decided we needed a lot more coordination, a lot more communication." GitHub added managers. The flat experiment ended.

Zappos implemented holacracy in 2013, replacing traditional hierarchy with self-organizing circles. The system had theoretical appeal—distributed authority, emergent coordination, no bosses to create bottlenecks. By 2015, thirty percent of the workforce had left. Exit interviews and internal surveys revealed the pattern: employees understood the system's mechanics but experienced strategic confusion. One employee captured the dysfunction: favoritism and management issues had somehow found power in the new system and worsened. The formal hierarchy was gone. The coordination problems remained, now handled by informal power structures that were less visible and less accountable than the managers they replaced.

Medium adopted holacracy in 2013 and abandoned it in 2016. Head of Operations Andy Doyle explained: "For larger initiatives, which require coordination across functions, it can be time-consuming and divisive to gain alignment." The system "began to exert a small but persistent tax on both our effectiveness, and our sense of connection to each other." The founder, Evan Williams, noted that recruiting the more experienced candidates had become difficult—who wants to join a bossless company, when career progression requires titles that translate to other organizations?

Buffer, the social media company famous for radical transparency, added management layers as it grew. The pattern repeated. Flat structures that enabled agility at fifty employees became coordination nightmares at one hundred fifty. The company chose function over ideology.

The cliff is Graicunas (1933) validated at organizational scale. Below one hundred people, informal coordination suffices because relationship counts remain tractable. Each person can maintain rough awareness of what others are doing. Shared lunches, chance hallway conversations, and tribal knowledge substitute for formal communication structures. Between one hundred and three hundred, the combinatorics cross a threshold. No individual can hold the whole organization in their head. Coordination that happened automatically now requires explicit structure. The choice is whether to add management layers deliberately or let shadow hierarchies emerge by default.

Shadow Hierarchies

Organizations that eliminate formal hierarchy do not eliminate hierarchy. They eliminate accountability for hierarchy.

Valve Corporation, the video game company, is famous for its flat structure. No managers. No job titles. Employees roll their desks to whatever project interests them. The company handbook, leaked and celebrated, describes a workplace where authority flows from competence and contribution rather than organizational position. The reality is different. Former employees describe a "hidden layer of powerful management structure" that operates beneath the official narrative. Decisions that matter—what games to ship, who gets bonuses, whose project gets resources—are made by a small group whose authority is real but unacknowledged. New employees learn quickly that some people's opinions matter more than others, that certain desks should not be rolled away from certain projects, that the freedom to choose your work is constrained by power dynamics that no handbook describes.

The pattern has a name. In 1972, political scientist Jo Freeman published "The Tyranny of Structurelessness," analyzing the dysfunction she observed in feminist organizations that rejected formal hierarchy as inherently oppressive. Her conclusion: "Contrary to what we would like to believe, there is no such thing as a structureless group. Any group of people of whatever nature that comes together for any length of time for any purpose will inevitably structure itself in some fashion." The question is whether structure is explicit and accountable or implicit and unaccountable.

Structurelessness favors the already powerful. When formal titles do not exist, informal influence determines outcomes. Those with more social capital—extroverts, people with external networks, those who match the demographic profile of existing power holders—accumulate authority that cannot be challenged because it is not officially recognized. Freeman observed that the most unstructured groups often become the most ruthlessly hierarchical, with power concentrated in friendship networks that outsiders cannot penetrate or even perceive.

Zappos discovered this under holacracy. The formal hierarchy was replaced with circles and lead links and governance meetings. The informal hierarchy was replaced with what employees described as high school dynamics. Popular kids emerged—people who had acquired power through social position rather than formal authority. The mechanisms of accountability that traditional management provides, however imperfect, had been removed. The mechanisms of influence that humans naturally create had not. The result was hierarchy with fewer constraints.

Valve cannot ship games on a predictable schedule. Zappos' website went unchanged for two years during the holacracy transition. These are the predictable consequences of removing formal coordination structures while humans continue to behave as humans. Difficult work that requires someone to be responsible does not get done when no one is formally responsible. Strategic priorities that require overriding individual preferences do not get addressed when no one has the authority to override. The shadow hierarchy handles what its members find interesting. Everything else waits.

The Hard Cap

Bain & Company (2010) maintains a database of organizational structures across one hundred twenty-five global companies. The pattern is consistent: best-in-class firms have no more than seven layers from CEO to frontline.

Average companies struggle with eight or nine. Beyond seven layers, information degradation accelerates, decisions slow exponentially, and bureaucratic paralysis sets in. The cap is the observed limit, documented across industries and decades.

The math explains why. Each layer is a compression event. Information traveling from frontline to executive passes through each layer, losing fidelity at every transition. The engineer's detailed technical explanation becomes the manager's summary, becomes the director's bullet points, becomes the VP's single sentence, becomes the executive's vague awareness that something is happening in that part of the organization. Seven compressions leave enough signal to make decisions. Eight or nine leave noise.

The same degradation operates in reverse. Strategic intent passes down through each layer, gaining specificity while losing context. The board's growth target becomes the CEO's revenue goal, becomes the VP's product launch, becomes the director's feature list, becomes the manager's sprint tickets, becomes the engineer's task. By the seventh compression, the connection between task and strategy is tenuous but traceable. By the ninth, the engineer is executing work whose purpose no one in their reporting chain can fully explain.

Large organizations do not break this cap. They reset it. General Electric under Jack Welch employed three hundred ten thousand people organized into thirteen business units. Each unit operated as its own hierarchy of four layers. The CEO sat atop the units as a coordination layer, not an additional management layer. Total depth: five operational layers, well under the cap. The structure scaled not by adding layers but by adding divisions, each respecting the geometric constraints that the research documents.

Berkshire Hathaway demonstrates the extreme case. Warren Buffett's corporate staff numbers twenty-five people. They coordinate sixty-plus subsidiaries employing over three hundred seventy thousand workers. The structure works because each subsidiary operates autonomously, with its own hierarchy. Corporate handles capital allocation and CEO selection. Everything else happens within divisions that maintain their own four-to-six layer structures. The hard cap is architecturally respected through a design that resets the count at each divisional boundary.

The implication is uncomfortable. Organizations cannot grow their way out of the Scale Trap. They can only restructure around it. A company that adds layers beyond seven is not scaling—it is degrading. The information loss compounds with each additional layer until decisions at the top bear no relationship to reality at the bottom and instructions from the top arrive at the bottom stripped of the context that would make them sensible. Organizations that ignore it discover the cost through dysfunction they struggle to diagnose, because the diagnosis requires information that the excess layers have already destroyed.

Why This Is Permanent

The Scale Trap cannot be eliminated because it emerges from geometry, not policy. You cannot maintain direct observation of one thousand people. You cannot track five thousand relationships. You cannot hold forty-seven contexts in working memory. These are constraints on the hardware running the organization—human brains with fixed cognitive limits operating in time that passes at one second per second.

Every proposed solution redistributes the problem, rather than solving it. Flat structures eliminate layers but do not eliminate coordination requirements; they push management work onto people without management authority, creating shadow hierarchies and coordination chaos. Technology extends reach but does not extend cognition; the manager with better dashboards can see more data but cannot process more relationships. Delegation distributes decisions but requires the delegator to monitor outcomes; the compression reappears as oversight rather than direct management.

The independence matters. Even if all teams had equal quality, scale would create compression. Even if all work were equally visible, scale would force information loss through hierarchical layers. Even if no legal pressure demanded documentation, scale would require representations that travel, while reality stays local. The other forces compound the damage, but scale alone is sufficient to guarantee that organizations past a certain size cannot see themselves accurately.

Consider the Engineering Director one final time. Give her teams of identical quality. Give her work that produces visible artifacts. Remove every legal requirement for documentation. She still cannot evaluate forty-seven people because she cannot observe forty-seven people. The performance reviews remain compressions of compressions. The strong performers remain unrecognized. The struggling engineers remain undiagnosed. The problem is not context or legibility or law. The problem is that human cognition does not scale and organizational size does.

This is the first proof. Scale operates as a structural force producing predictable dysfunction independent of implementation quality, cultural factors, or individual capability. The geometry is unforgiving. What follows is the second proof: what happens when strategic intent must cascade down through these same compression layers, losing context at every transition, until the people executing the work cannot see the reasoning that would let them execute it well.

CHAPTER 12

The Context Trap

The Staff Engineer receives the email on Monday morning. New product launch target: ship the customer dashboard redesign by the end of Q3. Marketing has already announced the feature in their roadmap deck. Sales is including it in enterprise pitches. Finance has baked the launch into quarterly guidance. The date is treated as fixed.

She reads the requirements. Six weeks of work, maybe eight, if nothing goes wrong. The target gives them twelve weeks, which looks generous on paper. She starts breaking down the technical approach, identifying dependencies, sketching the architecture. By Wednesday, she realizes the timeline is impossible.

The dashboard redesign requires migrating the data layer to the new schema. The schema migration cannot happen until the API versioning work is complete. The API versioning work is blocked on the authentication system refactor, which is three months behind schedule because two engineers left and their replacements are still ramping. Added together, the dependencies push the real timeline to six months, probably closer to eight, if nothing goes wrong.

She escalates to her manager. The manager escalates to the director. The director escalates to the VP. At each level, the message compresses. What starts as "we need six months because of three sequential dependencies that cannot be parallelized" arrives as "Engineering says they need more time." What starts as "the authentication refactor is behind because we lost institutional knowledge when two engineers left" arrives as "there are resourcing issues." The technical structure survives locally; only the summary survives the bottleneck.

The VP brings this to the executive team. The CTO explains that Engineering needs more time. The CFO points out that the launch is already in guidance and that moving it would ripple through forecasts. The CEO asks whether Engineering can find a way to make it work. The CTO commits to try. The VP tells the director to find a solution. The director tells the manager to get creative with prioritization. The manager tells the Engineer to figure out how to ship by the end of Q3.

The Engineer has three options. She can build the dashboard without the schema migration, implementing a temporary adapter layer that will need to be rewritten later. She can skip the API versioning, which would break existing integrations and require coordinated deployments with every client. She can skip proper authentication integration, leaving the dashboard with a separate login flow that ignores the permissions governing the rest of the system. All three options guarantee more labor and more risks than doing what it takes to do it right.

She chooses the first option. The dashboard ships on time and appears to work. Customers get the features they were promised; adoption numbers move in the right direction. Six months later, the technical debt from the adapter layer compounds into a scaling crisis that requires three engineers working full-time for two months to unwind. The cost of fixing the workaround exceeds the cost of building it correctly by a factor of four.

From the board's perspective, the launch is a success. Marketing hits its roadmap commitment. Sales closes deals using the new feature. Finance meets guidance. Engineering delivers on time. Within the frame they see, the decision to compress the timeline looks vindicated.

From the Engineer's perspective, the compression destroyed value. The dashboard could have been built correctly if given adequate time. The workaround was necessary only because the launch date was fixed before the technical reality was understood. The technical debt will slow future work, create maintenance burden, and eventually need to be paid down at much higher cost. Shipping on schedule saved twelve weeks and cost thirty.

The board has no instrument that surfaces this tradeoff. The twelve weeks saved appear cleanly in the quarterly results. The thirty lost weeks diffuse across future quarters, to be attributed to other factors, invisible in the metrics governance reviews. The compression happens at the point where strategic intent meets operational specifics. What is lost is the context that would make the tradeoff legible.

The Context Trap is the fact that strategic decisions must cascade through organizational layers to reach execution, and each layer compresses. The compression is cognitive necessity; human working memory cannot hold the full context at every level. But compression is lossy, and what is lost follows a pattern. Flexibility disappears. Risk tolerance vanishes. Tradeoffs become invisible. By the time strategic intent reaches the people who must execute it, the reasoning that would enable good local decisions has been stripped away.

The Engineer inherits a deadline without knowing whether it is absolute or negotiable, whether the strategy tolerates technical debt or forbids it, whether shipping late would be catastrophic or merely inconvenient. She is forced to guess, and when the guess is wrong, the organization pays a cost that never appears on any dashboard.

The Compression Mechanism

The compression in the opening scenario is cognitive necessity operating exactly as the system requires.

Human working memory holds approximately five to nine items at any moment. The limit is a measured constraint of the system, established through decades of cognitive research. John Sweller's (1988) research on cognitive load established that this bottleneck determines what any single mind can actively process. Exceed the limit and information displaces other information.

The executive attempting to hold the full technical context of the dashboard project—three sequential dependencies, authentication delays, institutional knowledge gaps, schema migration requirements—would saturate working memory and displace the strategic context their role requires: market positioning, competitive response, capital allocation, board expectations. The constraint is zero-sum. Context that enters pushes other context out.

The brain solves this problem through schema formation. A schema is a complex knowledge structure stored in long-term memory that working memory treats as a single item. The chess master sees a pattern that a novice would parse as dozens of individual pieces; the structure becomes one chunk, leaving working memory free for strategic calculation. Expertise arises from denser schemas.

Organizations build schemas the same way. The CEO manages the "Engineering" schema, a compressed representation containing five hundred engineers as a single cognitive unit. The schema is maintained by the VP of

Engineering, whose job is to ensure that complexity inside the organization remains encapsulated. When the VP reports to the CEO, they report schema-level information: "Engineering needs more time." The detail inside the schema—the dependency chain, the authentication delays, the institutional knowledge loss—stays inside. The schema is functioning as designed, preventing detail from leaking upward and overwhelming the executive layer.

The cybernetics literature formalizes this as variety attenuation. Ashby's (1956) law of requisite variety states that a controller can regulate a system only if the controller's variety matches or exceeds the system's variety. The frontline of a large organization generates enormous variety: thousands of customer interactions, countless technical decisions, continuous micro-adjustments to shifting conditions. The CEO has low variety by comparison; they can attend to only a handful of issues. If the CEO attempted to regulate the frontline directly, the mismatch would guarantee failure.

Hierarchy solves the mismatch through two operations. Moving upward, each layer attenuates variety. The engineer handles the specific dependency chain. The manager handles the team's capacity. The director handles the department's delivery timeline. The VP handles Engineering's alignment with the roadmap. By the time the signal reaches the CEO, millions of potential states have been compressed into a tractable report: on track or not on track, more resources needed or not. Moving downward, each layer amplifies variety. The CEO says "enter the European market." The VP translates this into initiatives. Directors translate the initiatives into projects. Managers translate the projects into tasks. The frontline performs the millions of actions required for execution.

The attenuation is where context dies. The Engineer's message contained the reasoning: three dependencies, specific technical constraints, institutional knowledge gaps. The message that survives attenuation contains only the conclusion: more time needed. The reasoning is the only information that would allow the executive team to evaluate the tradeoff—whether the timeline is worth the technical debt, whether the dependencies could be addressed differently, whether the schedule should flex. But reasoning is high-variety information. It does not survive the bottleneck. What survives is the low-variety summary that fits the cognitive constraints of the executive layer.

The mechanism operates as it must given the limits of human cognition and the mathematical requirements of controlling complex systems. The compression follows inevitably from those constraints. The loss is structural.

What Gets Lost

The compression mechanism does not strip information uniformly. Certain categories of context survive the bottleneck; others are systematically erased. The survival pattern is predictable because it follows from what hierarchy is built to preserve.

Goals survive. The dashboard must ship by Q3. Revenue must grow thirty percent. The European market must be entered. These are low-variety signals, already compressed to the form hierarchy can transmit.

Deadlines survive. Q3. End of fiscal year. Before the competitor launches. Temporal constraints require no additional context and no local interpretation. A deadline is the same instruction at every layer of the organization.

What does not survive is everything required for intelligent local adaptation.

Flexibility is the first casualty. The thirty-percent growth target had emerged from a planning process filled with assumptions about market conditions, competitive dynamics, and macroeconomic shifts. If those assumptions change, the target might change. The strategic layer knows this. Sensitivity analyses and scenario modeling reflected it. But the conditionality does not cascade. The engineer inheriting the Q3 deadline has no visibility into which assumptions would need to break before the deadline might flex. The date appears absolute because the assumptions were high-variety information and did not survive compression.

Risk tolerance is the second casualty. Every strategic choice carries implicit tolerance for failure. A board pursuing thirty-percent growth may expect that some initiatives will fail while others exceed expectations; the portfolio absorbs the variance. This tolerance is legible at the strategic layer, where the full distribution of bets is visible. It is invisible at the operational layer, where each initiative appears as an isolated commitment. The operational layer cannot calibrate its risk-taking because the organizational appetite recital never crosses the bottleneck.

Tradeoffs are the third casualty. The decision to pursue thirty-percent growth involved choosing growth over margin preservation, technical investment, market consolidation, or cultural stability. The reasoning was debated, documented, and decided. But the resulting rationale does not cascade. The Engineer deciding between shipping on time with technical debt or shipping late with clean architecture has no access to the tradeoff logic that would clarify which choice aligns with strategic preference. Only the deadline reaches her.

The pattern is consistent: what survives compression is what can be expressed in low-variety form—goals, deadlines, targets, metrics. What is lost is what requires high-variety transmission: the reasoning, the conditionality, the tolerance for deviation, the tradeoff logic. The information that survives is sufficient to describe the task.

The information that is lost is what would be required to execute it with judgment.

The loss is a structural consequence of transmitting complex intent through a bandwidth-limited channel. The executive layer cannot send the full context even if it attempts to, because the context is high-dimensional and the channel is narrow. What can be sent is what fits: the target without its reasoning, the deadline without its flexibility, the goal without its tradeoffs.

Why Calibration Fails

Organizations recognize the context gap and attempt to close it through communication: all-hands meetings, strategy documents, town halls, skip-levels, internal podcasts, leadership Slack channels. These mechanisms operate within the same bandwidth constraints they are trying to compensate for.

The all-hands meeting illustrates the problem. A CEO addressing two thousand employees has approximately forty-five minutes to convey strategic context. The audience spans functions, each facing different decisions, so each would benefit from knowing different contexts. The format requires communicating what applies broadly: the growth target, the competitive landscape, the quarterly results. The Engineer wondering whether her specific project justifies technical debt receives no clarity, because clarity at that resolution would require addressing hundreds of similar questions. The channel capacity determines what context can be transmitted.

Strategy documents face the same limitation from a different angle. A well-crafted strategy memo can explain why thirty-percent growth matters, what market opportunity it addresses, how it connects to long-term vision. This context is valuable and genuinely clarifying at the portfolio level. It does not answer the question the Engineer actually faces: whether the dashboard project is on the critical path or could be delayed, whether speed or sustainability matters more for this deliverable, whether the organization would accept a six-month timeline if the alternative is architectural debt. The document operates at the wrong resolution, providing portfolio-level reasoning to someone making project-level decisions. Bridging the gap would require transmitting the high-variety information that hierarchy compresses by design.

Town halls permit questions, which appears to address the problem. The Engineer could ask whether the dashboard timeline should flex given the dependency constraints. The format cannot scale to this use. Two thousand employees face context gaps; the session accommodates perhaps ten questions. Even when a specific question is asked, the answer must be given publicly, general enough to avoid creating precedents that would unravel coordination commitments across other teams.

Skip-level meetings offer higher bandwidth per interaction at the cost of coverage. A VP meeting directly with individual contributors can transmit nuanced context about strategic priorities, risk tolerance, tradeoff preferences. For those individuals, the context gap narrows. The mechanism reaches dozens; the organization contains thousands.

Each of these mechanisms attempts to push high-variety information through channels whose capacity is fixed. They reduce the severity of the context gap to a degree. They cannot eliminate it, because elimination would require expanding human cognitive bandwidth or reducing organizational complexity below the threshold where hierarchy becomes necessary. The constraint is architectural.

Mission Command: Distillation Done Right

The compression problem has been solved before, under conditions more demanding than quarterly targets. The solution is instructive because it accepts the constraint as given.

Nineteenth-century warfare outgrew centralized command. Armies had become too large, battlefields too dispersed, communication too slow for a commanding general to issue specific orders to every unit. By the time a courier reached a regiment with instructions, the tactical situation had changed. Orders optimized for conditions that no longer existed produced failure. The Prussian military recognized that the problem was structural: the variety of battlefield conditions exceeded the command channel's capacity to transmit specific responses.

Their solution was *Auftragstaktik*, now called Mission Command. The commander provides the intent behind the mission and the desired end state—why we are fighting and what success looks like—while explicitly withholding the method. A commanding general might issue a one-page order where previous doctrine required a hundred pages. The order specifies that a hill must be taken to protect the army's flank. It does not specify which approach to use, what time to attack, or how to respond to enemy counter-action. Those decisions belong to the officer on the ground, who has access to tactical conditions the general cannot see.

This is a documented compression algorithm. The high-variety information—tactical conditions, terrain, enemy disposition, unit readiness—stays at the layer where it exists. The low-variety information—strategic intent, desired outcome—is what crosses the bottleneck. The compression is deliberate and the loss is designed. What gets transmitted is the context required for intelligent local adaptation: the reasoning that makes good decisions possible, rather than the decisions themselves.

The approach requires institutional trust. The commanding general must trust that subordinate officers can translate intent into action without detailed guidance. Subordinate officers must trust that the intent is genuine—that they will not be punished for tactical decisions that honor the mission's purpose even if they deviate from what the general might have ordered. This trust is built through training, doctrine, and repeated demonstration. Without it, officers revert to waiting for specific orders, and the bandwidth constraint reasserts itself.

General Stanley McChrystal (2015) encountered a variant of this problem in Iraq. His task force faced a networked enemy that operated faster than traditional military hierarchy could respond. The insurgent network had no bandwidth constraints; information flowed laterally and decisions happened at the edge. McChrystal's hierarchy, optimized for a different kind of war, filtered information upward too aggressively. By the time intelligence reached decision-makers, the opportunity had passed.

McChrystal adjusted the compression ratio while preserving the command structure. The daily Operations and Intelligence briefing, previously a small meeting of senior leaders, expanded to include thousands of participants across the task force. The briefing transmitted strategic context—why specific targets mattered, how operations connected, what the broader campaign required—to people who had previously received only tactical assignments. Frontline operators still made tactical decisions, but now with access to strategic reasoning that standard hierarchy had been filtering out.

The insight was that traditional compression had become too aggressive for the operational environment. The hierarchy was transmitting goals while stripping the reasoning that would allow intelligent execution. Expanding who received the strategic briefing pushed more context further down the organization without disrupting the coordination structure. The hierarchy remained intact while the bandwidth for context increased.

Stafford Beer (1981) identified a related problem from cybernetic first principles. If hierarchy filters information as it travels upward, what happens when a frontline signal represents an existential threat rather than routine tactical noise? The filtering mechanism cannot distinguish between information that is safely compressed and information that must reach the top intact. A factory worker noticing a design flaw, a field officer observing enemy mobilization, an engineer discovering a critical vulnerability—these signals look like noise to the layers above because they originate at the wrong resolution. The hierarchy filters them by default.

Beer's solution was the algedonic channel: a dedicated pathway that bypasses normal compression to transmit survival-critical signals directly from the periphery to the center. The name comes from the Greek words for pain and pleasure—the channel carries only signals indicating danger or exceptional opportunity. Everything else travels through normal hierarchical compression. The algedonic channel operates parallel to hierarchy, compensating for hierarchy's specific structural weakness.

This architecture—hierarchy for routine compression, protected channels for exceptions—appears across effective organizations under different names. Whistleblower hotlines. Stop-the-line authority in manufacturing. Direct escalation paths for safety concerns. The common structure recognizes that hierarchical filtering is necessary for normal operations and insufficient for survival-critical signals.

The formal hierarchy provides coordination and accountability. The parallel channel provides adaptation and survival.

Why This Is Permanent

The preceding sections established the compression mechanism. What remains is to demonstrate that it operates independently of the other structural forces.

Consider the Staff Engineer facing the dashboard deadline, but grant her conditions that neutralize every other constraint this book has examined. Her manager has five direct reports, well within effective span of control. All her work is visible: no shadow systems, no informal channels, no unmeasured activity. No legal requirements shape her documentation or process. The organization has patient capital, a supportive board, leadership that genuinely wants good outcomes.

The Engineer still lacks what she needs to evaluate whether the Q3 deadline should flex.

The strategic intent behind the deadline—grow revenue thirty percent by expanding enterprise adoption—did not cascade with the target. What cascaded was the target itself: ship the dashboard by Q3. The reasoning that produced the target, the assumptions underlying it, the conditions under which it might change, the tradeoffs accepted to pursue it—all remained at the layer where the decision was made.

The compression operates through ordinary organizational function. The executive team conducting strategic planning cannot transmit the full context because the context is high-dimensional and human cognitive bandwidth is fixed. The CEO managing the "Engineering" schema cannot hold technical details of every project without displacing strategic context required for portfolio-level decisions. The VP summarizing Engineering capacity cannot include every dependency chain without overwhelming the receiving layer.

The compression accumulates through each handoff. The Engineer's manager summarizes three sequential dependencies as "engineering needs more time." At the director level, multiple such requests become "we're over-committed relative to capacity." The VP synthesizes departmental concerns for the CEO as "we need to prioritize." Each summary is accurate, and each strips the reasoning that would allow evaluation of the underlying tradeoff.

The result is that strategic context and decision authority distribute inversely. The CEO holds the reasoning behind the growth target—the assumptions, the tradeoffs, the conditions for flexibility. The Engineer holds the deadline and the technical constraints. The person making the implementation decision has the least access to the strategic context that would inform it.

Organizational interventions operate within the same bandwidth constraint they attempt to overcome. All-hands meetings cannot transmit strategic reasoning at the resolution required for thousands of individual decisions. Strategy documents cannot bridge portfolio logic and project execution. Skip-levels reach dozens when thousands face similar context gaps. Human cognition is the bottleneck, and management practices do not widen it.

This is the second structural force producing predictable organizational dysfunction. Scale creates the management layer trap, requiring hierarchical layers that compound the distance between decision and execution. Context creates the compression trap, degrading strategic intent as it travels downward and stripping the reasoning required for intelligent local adaptation. The two forces operate on different dimensions—span-of-control versus information bandwidth—and either alone is sufficient to produce the dysfunction.

The forces are independent. An organization can solve its span-of-control problems completely and still suffer context collapse. An organization can transmit strategic intent clearly to the first layer and watch it degrade through subsequent compressions. The traps compound but do not require each other. Each produces dysfunction that manifests as apparent incompetence, misalignment, or cultural failure, while remaining architectural in origin.

CHAPTER 13

The Legibility Trap

The forced ranking system is mathematically broken—fifty-three percent error rate, worse than random, provably flawed. But the brokenness distributes unevenly. The errors follow patterns. The system charges a tax, and the tax falls heaviest on work that resists the measurement frame.

The mechanism is structural. Systems that optimize for visibility systematically disadvantage contributions that resist quantification—prevention that manifests as absence, multiplication that diffuses across boundaries, judgment that cannot be codified, value that compounds over horizons longer than the measurement cycle. The system measures what is easy to measure and ignores what is hard to measure. The gap between actual contribution and measured contribution is the tax.

The Prevention Paradox

The site reliability engineer who prevents the outage produces no visible artifact. The system runs. Dashboards stay green. Alerts stay quiet. Customers experience no disruption. From the perspective of anyone reviewing performance, nothing happened. The year looks empty.

The adjacent engineer has a different year. Three major outages resolved. Two emergency deployments executed under pressure. Multiple late-night debugging sessions that saved customer data. The performance review glows with specific incidents, dramatic recoveries, measurable impact. Promotion is assured.

Prevention was more valuable. The outage that did not occur would have cost more if it did—in revenue, in customer trust, in engineering hours spent on recovery—than the outages that occurred and were resolved. The engineer who prevented the crisis created more value than the engineer who resolved the crisis. But prevention manifests as absence. Absence cannot be counted.

The pattern extends beyond site reliability. The security engineer who designs systems that resist penetration produces no incident reports. The quality engineer whose testing prevents bugs from reaching production generates no post-mortems. The architect whose capacity planning prevents scaling crises creates no heroic re-platforming stories. All prevention, all more valuable than response, all invisible in the metrics that drive performance evaluation.

When someone prevents failure, it is expected. The system was supposed to work. When someone responds to failure, it is heroic. They saved the day. Prevention costs you twice: once when doing work the business system cannot see, again when that invisibility determines your ranking.

The Multiplication Penalty

Someone documents the tribal knowledge before the senior engineer leaves. Someone notices when the junior engineer is struggling and creates space for questions. Someone mentors across teams, building capability that might not show up in their own metrics. Someone takes notes in the meeting so others can focus on the discussion. Someone remembers to celebrate the small wins that keep morale up during long projects.

Teams without this work are brittle. Knowledge doesn't exist in teams—only in individual heads—and disappears when experienced people leave. Junior engineers flounder without guidance. Cross-team collaboration fails. Meetings produce no actionable records. Morale collapses under sustained pressure. Connective work is valuable. That work is also invisible.

The value is multiplicative rather than additive. The mentor does not produce output; the mentor increases the output of everyone they touch. The documenter does not ship features; the documenter prevents the loss of capability that would slow every future feature. The coordinator does not close tickets; the coordinator reduces friction across the entire system. Multiplicative value diffuses. It shows up in other people's numbers, not in the multiplier's own metrics. In calibration, where individuals are ranked against individuals, diffuse value isn't tallied.

The penalty compounds because the work is both invisible and expected. In any functioning team, someone is doing connective work. If no one does it, the team degrades. But because the work is expected, doing it earns no special recognition. It is baseline. And because the work is invisible, not doing it often goes unnoticed until the consequences accumulate into crisis. The person who maintains the connective tissue of the organization is penalized for not doing visible individual work and not rewarded for doing invisible collective work.

The organization benefits. The calibration system does not value it. The gap between organizational benefit and individual recognition is the tax.

The Visibility Bind

Forced ranking requires self-promotion. You must make your contributions visible before and during calibration. Your manager is arguing for you against other managers arguing for their reports. If you have not equipped your manager with ammunition—specific achievements, quantifiable impact, compelling narratives—you will lose the political negotiation that determines your ranking.

Self-promotion is required. Self-promotion is also unevenly distributed as a skill.

Some people were socialized into it. They learned early that achievements must be claimed, that visibility must be cultivated, that the story of the work matters as much as the work itself. They catalog accomplishments naturally. They quantify impact instinctively. They build narratives around contributions without feeling awkward about it. For them, calibration is a game with learnable rules.

Others were socialized differently. They learned that the work should speak for itself, that claiming credit is unseemly, that good work will be recognized without self-advocacy. They underplay contributions because overplaying feels wrong. They assume their manager knows what they did because the manager was there. They arrive at calibration without ammunition because building ammunition felt like self-aggrandizement.

The system requires behavior it has not taught everyone to perform. The engineer who underplays contributions lacks ammunition for calibration. The manager cannot argue effectively because the evidence has not been provided. The ranking suffers not because performance was weak but because self-presentation was insufficient.

The bind extends across many dimensions. Introverts, people from cultures that de-emphasize individual achievement, people who entered the field through non-traditional paths and hadn't learned the professional etiquette, people whose previous organizations rewarded different behaviors—all face versions of the same structural disadvantage. The system measures performance filtered through self-presentation ability, and self-presentation ability is neither randomly distributed nor neutral with respect to who already holds power.

The Attribution Drift

Collaborative work gets attributed to whoever had the most visible role. Someone did the analysis; someone else presented it. The presenter is seen as the author. Someone wrote the code; someone else did the code review. In the retelling, it becomes the reviewer's architectural insight. Someone managed the project for six months; someone else escalated the critical blocker in week twenty-two. The escalator is remembered as having saved it.

None of this requires malice. Visibility determines credit, and visibility correlates with existing credibility. Those who already have credibility receive credit more easily— their contributions are noticed, remembered, attributed correctly. Those who lack credibility must work harder to receive the same recognition. A contribution from someone already seen as a leader is coded as leadership. The same contribution from someone not yet seen as a leader is coded as support work or as intrusion.

The system measures visible credit rather than actual contribution. The measurement error is systematic. Over time, the engineer whose contributions are consistently under-attributed develops a thin track record. The engineer whose contributions are consistently over-attributed develops an impressive one. Calibration reflects the recorded contributions rather than the actual contributions. The gap between what was produced and what was credited is the tax.

The Compounding Effect

Each of these mechanisms—prevention undervalued, multiplication invisible, self-promotion unevenly distributed, attribution drifting toward the already-credible—operates independently. Together, they compound.

An engineer who excels at prevention, who performs substantial multiplicative work, who was not socialized into self-promotion, and whose contributions are routinely under-attributed will land in the bottom of forced rankings despite his actual performance being equal to or exceeding colleagues who rank higher. The system measures performance filtered through legibility, and legibility is systematically biased toward certain kinds of work and certain kinds of presentation.

The bias is structural rather than individual. The manager running the calibration may genuinely believe they are being objective. They are working with the information they have—the visible achievements, the compelling self-narratives, the contributions that were assertively claimed and clearly attributed. The information itself is biased. The legibility system produced biased information. The calibration optimizes within that bias. The outcome is biased even when every individual actor is attempting fairness.

And the bias compounds over time. The engineer who lands in the bottom rankings once learns the system penalizes their work style. They adapt—maybe by doing less prevention and more visible response work, maybe by doing less multiplication and more individual contribution, maybe by leaving for an organization where their contributions are valued. Each adaptation is individually rational. The aggregate effect is organizational degradation.

The organization loses the prevention that kept its systems stable. The organization loses the multiplicative work that built capability and retained knowledge. The organization loses people who see what the dominant frame erases. The next generation watches. They see quiet competence culled, while loud mediocrity advances. They learn what is valued and what is punished. They leave earlier, or they never join at all.

The Strategic Cost

The organization loses individuals. More importantly, it loses perspectives. The people most disadvantaged by legibility systems are often the people who see what those systems erase. The engineer who does prevention sees risks before they become crises. The engineer who does multiplicative work sees capability gaps before they become failures. The engineer who notices attribution drift sees when credit systems are misattributing value.

These are the capabilities organizations need most when navigating uncertainty, when adapting to change, when building for the long term rather than optimizing for the short term. Legibility systems consistently select against these capabilities by selecting against the people who embody them.

The cost is counterfactual. The organization does not know what the engineer who left would have prevented, what the never-hired candidate would have built, what perspectives were lost when the calibration system culled people who saw what the metrics missed. The absence cannot be measured. The loss is real.

And the loss is permanent. Once the capability is gone, the organization cannot recognize what it has lost because the team's capability to recognize the gap also left with the individuals who had it. The metrics show everything is fine. The projects ship on time. The calibrations proceed smoothly. The erosion is invisible until it is catastrophic.

The Pattern Beyond Forced Ranking

Forced ranking is one instance. Every legibility system creates versions of the same tax.

Cost-center accounting erases the platform team's multiplicative value—the value manifests in what other teams can build rather than in direct output. The platform team's work is preventive, infrastructural, enabling. The metrics count expense. The tax falls on teams doing invisible work.

Go-getter cultures reward visibility over craft—the engineer who ships fast and talks loudly gets promoted over the engineer who builds correctly and works quietly. The metrics count velocity and volume. The tax falls on people whose excellence is depth rather than speed.

Supervisor interventions erase local expertise—the worker who has accumulated tacit knowledge is overridden by global procedures. The procedures are visible and defensible. The expertise is invisible. The tax falls on people whose knowledge cannot be codified.

Engineering timelines suppress variance—the promise to ship by a given date requires cutting the exploration that would have produced better outcomes. The timeline is visible and binding. The quality is invisible until failure. The tax falls on engineers who see what the timeline erases.

Every legibility system charges the same tax: if your value does not project onto the measurement frame, if your work resists quantification, if your contribution is preventive rather than responsive, multiplicative rather than additive, tacit rather than explicit, long-horizon rather than short-horizon—you pay.

Why This Matters for the Cage Framework

The legibility tax proves the Cage operates at human scale. The same physics that compressed strategic language in 10-Ks now compresses careers. Fiduciary duty demands demonstrable soundness. Demonstrable soundness privileges what can be shown. What can be shown is a subset of what matters. The system optimizes for what can be shown. The optimization is systematically incomplete.

Organizations cannot fix this through better calibration or more training or stronger values statements. The problem is structural. Legibility systems will always privilege visible work over invisible work, because visibility is what makes work legible. Wherever invisible work exists, legibility systems will undervalue it. Whoever does that work will pay the tax.

The tax is physics. It is the predictable consequence of optimizing for what formal systems can capture, while ignoring what they erase. The tax is real. The tax is systematic. The tax compounds. And the work that pays it most—prevention, multiplication, tacit judgment, long-horizon investment—is precisely the work organizations can least afford to lose.

The Cage is inefficient. It destroys value it cannot see. The proof is complete. The pattern is clear. Now we show how law amplifies these forces, crystallizing organizational pressure into binding requirement.

CHAPTER 14

The Fiduciary Trap

The Senior Director at Apple watched the keynote with a knot in his stomach. Tim Cook was on stage describing Vision Pro's revolutionary spatial computing capabilities. The audience gasped at the demos. The press would call it magical. The stock would rise. And the director knew—with the certainty that comes from having been in the room where the product actually was—that what Tim Cook was describing did not yet exist in shippable form.

The demos were real. The technology worked under controlled conditions. But production-ready? No. The thermal management failed under sustained load. The battery life hit spec only with usage patterns no actual customer would follow. The interface had enough latency that extended use caused nausea in thirty percent of internal testers. These were solvable problems. They required time—eighteen months of iteration, maybe twenty-four to get it right.

The keynote had just committed to shipping in six months.

He knew what would happen next. Engineering would be told the timeline was fixed. Marketing had made

179

promises. Finance had baked the launch into guidance. The board had approved the roadmap. The question would be "what can we cut to ship on time", rather than "do we have time to build it correctly." Thermal management would get deferred to a future update. Battery optimization would ship "good enough", with software improvements promised later. The latency would be addressed through careful demo choreography and user education about "proper usage patterns."

They would ship. The reviews would be mixed. The price would be justified by calling it "first generation" and "developer-focused." Customers would buy it because it was Apple, then quietly stop using it because the experience did not match the promise. And from the board's perspective, from counsel's perspective, from the perspective of fiduciary duty and quarterly guidance and demonstration of prudent execution, every decision along the way would be defensible.

This is the Fiduciary Trap at product scale. Billions in development costs, years of engineering effort, products that could have been excellent—all compromised not by technical failure but by legal structures that make variance dangerous and smoothness mandatory.

The Variance Problem

Waste doctrine creates legal pressure toward market-rate conformity and away from outlier decisions. But the doctrine's effect is subtler and more pervasive than just converging toward conventional executive compensation or industry-standard practices. Waste doctrine creates systematic pressure to prefer smooth returns over jagged returns, even when jagged returns have higher expected value.

Consider two product strategies over five years. Strategy A delivers consistent incremental improvements: ten percent revenue growth each year, steady margin expansion, predictable quarterly results that meet guidance. Strategy B is volatile: two years of investment with no revenue, followed by explosive growth that doubles the business, followed by consolidation, followed by another breakthrough. By year five, Strategy B produces three times Strategy A's total value creation. From a long-term shareholder perspective, Strategy B is obviously superior.

From a fiduciary duty perspective under the business judgment rule, Strategy A is safer. Strategy A never creates a moment where directors must explain to shareholders, to plaintiffs' counsel, or to judges reviewing their decisions after the fact why they tolerated periods of declining results, why they continued funding projects that were not showing returns, why they accepted volatility when competitors were delivering predictability. Every quarterly earnings call for Strategy A is a demonstration of sound stewardship. Strategy B creates quarterly earnings calls where directors must explain gaps between expectations and reality, must defend decisions to continue investing through downturns, must justify variance that looks like loss of control.

The business judgment rule protects both strategies if the process was sound. But the exposure differs. Strategy A is never challenged because smoothness itself signals control. Strategy B invites challenge at every trough. Each moment of underperformance becomes a datapoint that plaintiffs can use to argue the directors were not adequately informed, were not exercising proper oversight, were not meeting their duty of care. The directors may ultimately prevail—the business judgment rule is strong—but they must periodically defend themselves. Strategy A directors never face that scrutiny because the smoothness preempts the challenge.

Rational directors, facing this asymmetry, prefer Strategy A, even when they intellectually understand Strategy B creates more value. The legal exposure from variance exceeds the return from value creation when directors are the ones bearing the liability risk, while shareholders capture the upside.

Legal structures create asymmetric payoffs. The director who delivers smooth mediocrity faces minimal legal risk. The director who delivers jagged excellence faces quarterly scrutiny, potential activist pressure, and litigation risk at every trough. The rational strategy is to optimize for smoothness rather than for total value creation.

Product development inherits this pressure. The moonshot that might produce breakthrough but will definitely produce variance gets shaped, scoped, and compromised until it looks smooth enough to be defensible. The shaping is structurally adapted to legal exposure, rather than malicious.

Vision Pro: When Variance Cannot Be Hidden

Vision Pro was announced in June 2023 and shipped in February 2024. The eight-month development window was impossibly tight for a first-generation product category. Everyone inside Apple knew this. The product required solving problems no one had solved at consumer scale: high-resolution displays with minimal latency, precise eye tracking, natural gesture recognition, thermal management in a head-mounted form factor, battery life sufficient for meaningful usage.

Apple had the technical capability to solve these problems. Given time. The question was whether they had time within the committed timeline. They did not. So the product that shipped was the product that could be defended within the timeline constraint, rather than the product the novel technology deserved.

The reviews reflected this. The display quality was praised. The eye tracking was impressive. But the weight made extended use uncomfortable. The battery lasted two hours, requiring tethered operation for any meaningful work session. The app ecosystem was sparse. The use cases were unclear. The price of three thousand five hundred dollars could not be justified by the limited functionality. Sales were far below internal projections.

From a product perspective, failure. From a fiduciary perspective, defensible. Apple announced the product category, demonstrated technical leadership, shipped within the committed timeline, and established a platform for future development. The board approved the investment based on strategic positioning rather than near-term returns. The execution followed the approved process. No one can argue the directors were uninformed or that the decision was irrational. The product's commercial disappointment does not create legal liability because the process was sound.

But from an engineering perspective, tragedy. The team knew what would be required to ship a great product. They had prototypes that worked better but were not production-ready within the timeline. They had roadmaps that would have produced a compelling second-generation device. They made the compromises necessary to ship within the announced timeline, knowing those compromises would limit adoption, knowing they were building a product that would not fulfill its potential, knowing they were burning billions of dollars to hit a date that was set before the technical reality was understood.

The timeline was set by strategic positioning requirements, which were themselves driven by quarterly narrative needs, rather than by technical requirements. Apple needed to demonstrate continued innovation leadership. The Vision Pro announcement served that need. The product had to ship within a time frame that made the announcement credible. Eight months was what the timeline allowed. The product that shipped was the product that could be built in eight months, rather than the product that could have been built with adequate time.

This is the asynchronous lie at flagship scale. Marketing operates in narrative time—keynotes, quarterly guidance, the rhythm of analysts' expectations. Engineering operates in discovery time—the irreducible duration required to solve problems no one has solved before. Vision Pro shipped when narrative time demanded it. Discovery time needed another year. The product that shipped was the product that narrative time allowed.

Apple Intelligence: Shipping Broken to Meet Guidance

Apple Intelligence was announced at WWDC 2024 as a foundational AI capability integrated across the operating system. The demonstrations showed Siri understanding context, proactively suggesting actions, drafting emails, summarizing notifications. The pitch was that Apple's privacy-first approach and on-device processing would deliver AI capabilities without compromising user data.

The product that shipped in iOS 18.1 bore little resemblance to what was demonstrated at the event. Siri remained frustratingly limited. The context understanding was shallow. The proactive suggestions were generic. The email drafting was so unreliable that most users disabled it. The notification summaries occasionally worked but frequently produced nonsensical results. The promise was intelligence. The reality was gimmick.

Apple's response was that these were "first-generation" features that would improve over time through software updates. This framing is technically accurate and strategically necessary. Shipping broken and fixing later is what happens when the announcement timeline is determined by competitive positioning, and product reality is determined by technical difficulty.

The competitive pressure was real. Google and Microsoft had shipped AI features. Apple's market position in premium devices depends on being perceived as technically leading rather than following. The WWDC announcement was strategically necessary. The capabilities demonstrated were not technically ready for mass deployment. The gap between announcement and reality was bridged by shipping what could be built within the timeline and promising that updates would close the distance.

From a fiduciary perspective, rational. The strategic risk of being perceived as behind in AI exceeds the execution risk of shipping features that underdeliver. The announcement maintains market position. The gradual improvement through updates is defensible as iterative development. The board approved the roadmap based on competitive positioning needs. The execution followed the approved strategy.

From an engineering perspective, another compromise forced by timeline pressure. The team knew the capabilities demonstrated at WWDC required more development time. They built what could be shipped within the iOS release cycle. They accepted that their initial release would disappoint users, in exchange for hitting the announced timeline. They prioritized demonstrating progress over delivering quality because the demonstration was strategically necessary and the quality could be addressed in updates.

The pattern is consistent across both products: strategic positioning demands announcement, announcement creates timeline commitment, timeline commitment forces engineering concession, concession results in products that ship broken or incomplete, brokenness is defended as "first generation" or "iterative development." The individual decisions are rational. The cumulative effect is systematic delivery of products that do not fulfill their potential because technical reality cannot match the timeline demands that competitive positioning requires.

Google Glass: When the Officer Gap Kills Execution

Google Glass launched in 2013 as an Explorer Program, positioning the device as experimental hardware for early adopters. The positioning was careful—a limited release to gather feedback and iterate on it, rather than a consumer product launch. The board approved the project as a research initiative with long-term strategic value in wearable computing.

The device was technically impressive. The display worked. The voice commands functioned. The camera captured reasonable quality video. But the product was not ready for any meaningful scale. The battery lasted hours rather than days. The user interface was awkward. The social dynamics were terrible—people wearing Glass were mocked, banned from establishments, and perceived as invasive. The privacy concerns were legitimate and unaddressed.

Google continued the program for two years, then shut it down. The official narrative was that Glass was always an experiment, that the learnings were valuable, that the technology would be applied elsewhere. This narrative protects the board's decision to fund the project. The board can point to the strategic rationale, the measured approach through the Explorer Program, the decision to shut down when commercial viability was unclear. The business judgment rule protects this process.

But internally, the story was different. The team wanted more time to solve the fundamental problems—battery life, social acceptability, clear use cases. They had roadmaps for second- and third-generation devices that would address the shortcomings. They believed the category had long-term potential but needed patient iteration, without the pressure of commercial launch timelines.

The pressure came anyway. Media coverage created expectations. The Explorer Program generated publicity that made Glass feel like a consumer product rather than a research project. Internal stakeholders wanted to see returns. The ambiguity about whether Glass was research or product created tension. Eventually, the project was shut down because the execution could not satisfy the expectations the initial publicity had created, rather than because the technology failed.

This is the officer gap operating in product development. The board approved Glass as a research initiative—protected by the business judgment rule, insulated by the strategic positioning, defensible as long-term investment in wearable computing. But the executives managing the project faced different pressures. They lacked the statutory shield directors enjoy. The publicity created expectations they could not control. The ambiguous positioning between research and product made every decision contestable.

The result was execution that could not fully commit to either research or product. Too much pressure to show progress for pure research. Too many fundamental problems for market-ready product launch. The project existed in the gap where the board's strategic patience and the executives' tactical exposure created contradictory demands that made success impossible.

The Pattern Revealed

The pattern across Vision Pro, Apple Intelligence, and Google Glass is identical to the pattern across all moonshots that die in the Cage. The board approves bold strategic vision—protected by the business judgment rule as long as the decision process appears informed and good-faith. The executives responsible for execution face different constraints—they lack the statutory protections; they must deliver results within timelines that demonstrate progress; they cannot fully commit to uncertain long-horizon work when their personal liability and career prospects depend on demonstrable outcomes within reach.

The boldness dies in translation from boardroom to operating reality, but not because executives are timid or engineers are incompetent or anyone lacks vision. The legal structure creates asymmetric exposure, where directors are protected for bold decisions, while officers and engineers bear the consequences when bold decisions produce variance.

The compromise is structural. The board approves the moonshot. Marketing announces it. Executives inherit a timeline derived from strategic positioning rather than technical reality. Engineers build what can be shipped within that timeline. The product launches compromised. The compromise is defended as "first generation" or "iterative development" or "research program." The defense is effective—no one faces legal liability; no one's career is destroyed; the strategic positioning is maintained. The moonshot becomes a compromised launch that delivers some fraction of its potential, while burning resources that could have produced breakthroughs if given adequate time.

The waste is counterfactual. Vision Pro shipped and generated revenue. Apple Intelligence shipped and demonstrated AI capability. Glass shut down but produced learnings. From a legal perspective, no waste occurred—the decisions were informed; the processes were sound; the outcomes were defensible even if disappointing.

From a capability perspective, billions of dollars and years of engineering effort created products that did not fulfill their potential because legal structures made variance dangerous and smoothness mandatory.

Why This Matters for the Cage Framework

The moonshot autopsies prove that the Fiduciary Trap operates on actual products with measurable consequences, rather than just in abstract governance. Vision Pro's compromised launch cost Apple billions in development, production, and opportunity cost. Apple Intelligence's under-delivery damages Apple's reputation for polish and quality. Glass's eventual shutdown wasted years of research and engineering effort.

These are flagship products from the world's most valuable and most admired technology companies, rather than edge cases. If Apple and Google cannot protect moonshots from variance-suppressing legal pressure, what chance do other organizations have?

The trap is structural. Apple has patient capital, visionary leadership, technical excellence, and market position. Google has similar advantages. None of that prevents the Fiduciary Trap from operating, because it operates through legal architecture, not decisions or culture. Variance is legally dangerous even when variance creates value.

The proof is complete. Convergence operates through mathematical necessity—forced ranking produces systematic errors because scale, context, and legibility forces compound. The Scale Trap operates through geometric constraints—span-of-control limits create compression even without other forces. The Context Trap operates through cascade compression—strategic intent is lost as abstraction becomes specification. The Legibility Trap operates through systematic bias—systems optimizing for visibility always disadvantage people doing invisible work. The Fiduciary Trap operates through legal pressure creating asymmetric exposure—directors protected for bold decisions, officers exposed for variance, engineers inheriting impossible timelines, bold moonshots compromised to maintain smoothness.

The question is what you build once you see it.

CHAPTER 15

The Cage Everywhere

The Cage everywhere. Each pattern follows the same physics: formal systems compress reality into manageable representations; the compression is systematically lossy; organizations optimize for what survives compression. Once you see it, you cannot unsee it.

Marketing Timeline > Engineering Timeline

External commitments set internal constraints. The keynote date, the earnings guidance, the board deck—these become fixed points. Engineering inherits a constraint that was set in a different universe. The gap between commitment and capability is where quality dies. *The CRM vendor promises "AI-powered forecasting" at the user conference. Engineering learns the date from the press release. The feature ships with a linear regression labeled "AI."*

Heroic Recovery > Preventive Design

Response generates artifacts. Prevention generates silence. The 3 a.m. incident response produces post-mortems, Slack threads, grateful emails from leadership. The quarter spent hardening the system produces green dashboards no one looks at. Formal systems need events to reward. They reward the visible save over the invisible design that would have made saving unnecessary. *The engineer who catches the memory leak in production gets the spot bonus. The engineer who wrote the memory-safe implementation that never leaked gets "meets expectations."*

Cost Reduction > Value Creation

Expense is visible in one column. Value is scattered, indirect, often counterfactual. When formal systems cannot represent multiplicative value—the platform that makes seventy teams faster, the prevention that avoids the outage—they optimize for what they can see. Headcount becomes the target. The value destroyed was real but unmeasured. *The internal tools team is cut. Each product team now builds its own deployment scripts. Total engineering hours increase. The savings appear on one ledger; the cost is distributed across dozens.*

Promises & Ruthless Prioritization > Responsible Scoping

Commitments are made before estimates. Sales, Marketing, Finance, and the board encode the promise. Engineering inherits the gap. The promise is external and legible; the scoping is internal and invisible. Boards see whether commitments were met, not which corners were cut. When scope exceeds timeline, scope gets cut—but the commitment stays intact. "Ruthless prioritization" is often a flattering name for structural over-commitment. *The feature is promised in six months. The estimate is nine. Leadership chooses "MVP." The MVP ships without the capabilities customers were promised. Support tickets spike. The next quarter is spent on "fast follows."*

Visible Activity > Actual Progress

When progress must be demonstrated through formal tracking, effort shifts from work to demonstration. Velocity metrics require tickets. Tickets require chunking. Work that doesn't chunk—architecture, exploration, deep debugging—gets deferred. The ceremony becomes the work. *The team completes 47 story points. The system is no more stable than last sprint. But the burndown chart looks excellent.*

Narrative Continuity > System Reliability

The quarterly story must be smooth. Accounting choices flatten revenue. Marketing spend is timed to guidance. Operational issues are minimized in the script. Meanwhile, infrastructure stretches, technical debt accumulates, and the investment that would prevent future crises is denied because it would hurt this quarter's margin. The broken product can be fixed. The missed guidance cannot. The system behaves accordingly. *The earnings call reports record growth. The on-call rotation is burning out. The board sees the first; the second has no slide.*

Process Accumulation (The Ratchet)

Each new control is individually defensible. The breach triggers security procedures. The failed launch triggers readiness reviews. The audit finding triggers more documentation requirements. Every added control can be shown to an auditor; the absence of controls cannot. Twenty years later, there are hundreds of procedures, thousands of approval gates. No single one can be removed—each addresses a real risk, has sponsorship, is embedded in compliance. The ratchet only tightens. *A deploy that took one approval in 2015 now requires seven. Each approval was added after an incident. No incident justified removing one.*

Standardization > Local Expertise

Global procedures are auditable. Local expertise is tacit. When they conflict, the procedure wins—it can be shown to regulators, documented for new hires, defended to leadership. What is lost is exactly what made the work excellent: the variance, the judgment, the adaptation to context. *The new ticketing system requires categorization before routing. The veteran support rep who knew which engineer to ping directly now waits in the queue like everyone else.*

Short-Term Optics > Long-Term Capability

The math is done in quarters, not decades. The buyback raises earnings per share. The R&D cut improves margin. Executives hit compensation targets. Analysts praise discipline. Five years later, the product line is stale and competitors have moved ahead. Fiduciary duty to current shareholders optimizes for current shareholders—who will be gone before the consequences arrive. *The company announces a ten billion dollar buyback. The advanced research lab is closed. The stock rises four percent The technology they were developing appears in a competitor's product three years later.*

The Pattern Made Explicit

One pattern repeats across domains. Formal systems must compress reality into manageable representations. The compression is systematically lossy. What gets lost are the dimensions that do not fit the frame—prevention, expertise, quality, long-term capability, multiplicative value, tacit knowledge. Organizations optimizing for what the frames capture systematically destroy what the frames erase.

The destruction is geometric—the inevitable consequence of navigating by incomplete maps while pretending the maps are complete. It happens in Engineering timelines and forced rankings and cost-center accounting and product commitments and process accumulation and every other domain where formal systems meet organizational reality.

The proof is complete. You have seen it mathematically, seen who pays, seen it across domains. The Cage is physics. It is the systematic, predictable consequence of four forces meeting: scale demanding compression because coordination requires it, context hiding strategic intent as abstraction becomes specification, legibility privileging what can be demonstrated over what creates value, law amplifying all three by making defensible process safer than correct judgment.

The question is what you build once you see it clearly.

Further Patterns

The geometry described in this book appears wherever formal systems grow complex enough to matter. What follows are situations observed in the wild. They are not case studies with lessons. They are territories where the physics operates. The reader who has absorbed the framework will recognize the forces. What to make of them is yours.

Each territory that follows shows the same geometry. Wherever Mode B appears—Apple under Jobs, Bridgewater under Dalio, SpaceX under concentrated private control—it exists because some forcing function is spending energy to hold the system away from its Mode A equilibrium. The moment those forcing functions weaken—Jobs dies, Dalio steps back, voting control dilutes, regulatory or fiduciary pressure intensifies—the system does not evolve. It reverts. Variance shrinks. Product truth yields to schedule. Radical norms soften into conventional ones. The Cage reasserts itself.

The question is not whether reversion will happen. The question is whether the organization extracted irreversible progress while the window was open, and whether the reversion was designed or accidental.

Apple Under Jobs

Steve Jobs maintained Mode B operation inside a public company for nearly fifteen years after his return to Apple in 1997. The conditions were specific: personal authority that made board challenge costly, a track record that bought tolerance for variance, and a willingness to accept quarters that disappointed Wall Street in service of product truth.

The authority was not incidental. Jobs's personal brand was Apple's brand. Removing him again would have damaged Apple more than tolerating his methods damaged the board's sense of procedural propriety. So the board tolerated the variance he cultivated, which fiduciary duty would normally have forbidden. He could delay products that weren't ready, even when it meant missing the Christmas quarter. He could kill profitable lines. He could say no to analysts who wanted guidance.

While that window was open, Apple extracted structural artifacts: an ecosystem that locks in users across devices, a supply chain that competitors cannot replicate, a retail presence that made the brand tangible, a design language that became industry grammar. These persist and do not require Jobs to maintain them. The variance that created them did not transfer to his successors.

When Jobs died, Apple began drifting toward Mode A. The post-Jobs era produced Vision Pro shipped before its technology matured, Apple Intelligence released before it worked, and iPhone cycles defined by schedule rather than readiness. The forcing function had been removed, and the system reverted toward its equilibrium.

Bridgewater's Radical Transparency

Ray Dalio built Bridgewater Associates around an explicit attempt to institutionalize external perspective. Meetings were recorded. Disagreement was mandatory. Anyone could challenge any decision regardless of hierarchy. The system created and enforced formal mechanisms for what most organizations leave informal—the capacity to tell leadership they are wrong.

For decades, it worked. Bridgewater maintained strategic variance that conventional asset managers could not. The fund outperformed during periods when standard approaches failed. The radical transparency created genuine external perspective by making frame challenging procedurally required rather than culturally tolerated.

The limitations emerged as Dalio stepped back. Reports suggest the culture moderated toward conventional forms. The discomfort of radical transparency—being recorded, being challenged, having your errors made visible—requires continuous energy to maintain. Most people, given the choice, prefer comfort. Without the founder's authority enforcing the norms, the norms softened.

SpaceX and Structural Protection

SpaceX operates under conditions that weaken three of the four Cage forces simultaneously. Private ownership eliminates most fiduciary pressure. Concentrated control—Musk's voting authority—eliminates board constraint. Fast feedback loops—rockets either work or they explode—make Mode A's narrative smoothing obviously false within minutes of a launch.

The result is tolerance for variance that public companies cannot sustain. SpaceX attempts launches that fail publicly, iterates rapidly on the failures, and makes decisions that would trigger shareholder litigation in a different ownership structure. The Starship program—repeated explosive failures, each teaching something—would be impossible under quarterly earnings pressure. The failures would require explanation. The explanations would invite challenge. The challenge would create pressure toward safer, slower, more defensible approaches.

The conditions are not replicable for most organizations. Private ownership with patient capital is rare. Concentrated control is rarer. Feedback loops that immediately punish Mode A are industry-specific. But the case demonstrates that the Cage's intensity varies with structure. The

forces are not uniform. They can be weakened by design—
if you control the design.

Boeing's Long Drift

For decades, Boeing's engineering culture was the forcing
function. The company that built the 707 and the 747
operated on a principle that engineers could override
schedule when safety or quality demanded it. The culture
was institutional identity, unwritten but binding. Engineers
had authority because engineering judgment had built the
company. That authority produced aircraft that defined
commercial aviation and safety records that justified the
deference.

Boeing merged with McDonnell Douglas in 1997. The
merger was structured as Boeing acquiring McDonnell
Douglas, but McDonnell Douglas executives came to
dominate the combined company's leadership. The engineering culture that had defined Boeing began to erode.

The erosion took decades. Headquarters moved from
Seattle to Chicago in 2001, away from the factory floor.
Financial metrics gradually rose in priority relative to engineering judgment. The 787 Dreamliner program outsourced
design and manufacturing to a degree unprecedented for
Boeing. By the time the 737 MAX entered development,
schedule pressure dominated engineering discretion.

MCAS was a solution to an aerodynamic problem
created by fitting larger engines onto an aging airframe.
The business requirement shaped the engineering approach:
a new aircraft would take too long, so Boeing modified
the 737 to ship faster. The modification created handling
characteristics that required software compensation. The
software had failure modes that were not adequately communicated to pilots, and two crashes killed 346 people.

While engineering authority held, Boeing extracted aircraft that still fly, safety protocols that became industry standard, and a reputation built over decades. The forcing function's removal revealed how dependent those achievements had been on the culture that created them.

The NHS and Target Culture

Before the reforms, the British National Health Service operated on clinical judgment. Doctors and nurses made decisions based on patient need, professional training, and institutional knowledge passed through practice. The system was inefficient, opaque to administrators, and impossible to audit at scale. It was also functional. Care happened because clinicians decided it should. The system built institutional knowledge, training pipelines, and professional accountability that formal metrics would later displace.

Britain's National Health Service in the 2000s became a laboratory for target-driven management. Wait times were measured. Targets were set. Performance against targets determined funding and leadership tenure.

Measured wait times fell, though the underlying reality diverged from the measurements. The system learned to satisfy the measurement rather than the intent. Patients were kept in ambulances to avoid starting the wait-time clock, moved to trolleys in corridors that technically counted as "admitted," and reclassified into categories with different targets.

The most severe consequence emerged at Mid Staffordshire NHS Foundation Trust, where target pressure contributed to conditions that led to hundreds of excess deaths. Staff were stretched thin. Complaints were ignored. The metrics remained within acceptable ranges throughout the period of decline. The formal system's legibility requirements were satisfied as the underlying function failed.

GE's Long Unwinding

General Electric under Jack Welch became the model for a generation of management practice. Forced ranking. Six Sigma. Continuous restructuring. The stock price rose for twenty years. Business schools taught the methods as proven science.

The critique is not of statistical process control itself—Deming's insight (1986) that systems produce variation, and that most variation is structural rather than individual, remains essential. The critique is of what happens when methods designed to stabilize manufacturing processes become instruments for managing knowledge work, and when metric achievement displaces the judgment those metrics were meant to inform.

The methods had costs that did not appear on the timeline Welch occupied. Infrastructure maintenance was deferred. Institutional knowledge was culled, alongside "bottom performers." GE Capital grew to dominate the company's profits, masking erosion in the industrial businesses. The system optimized for metrics Welch could see during his tenure. The metrics he could not see—capability depth, infrastructure integrity, knowledge retention—degraded invisibly.

By 2018, GE had lost over eighty percent of its peak market value. The businesses Welch had "optimized" required decades of rebuilding. The forced ranking he had championed was abandoned by most companies that had adopted it. The "management science" proved to be selection bias at scale—methods that appeared to work during a bull market, applied by a leader whose tenure ended before the consequences arrived.

The Cage

Human resources. At some point the noun and the adjective switched places. Humans became the modifier; resource became the thing. The phrase tells us what we need to know about how organizations see people: inputs to be optimized, costs to be managed, units to be allocated. The language is honest. The discomfort it provokes is the discomfort of recognition.

Consider the leadership interview. The candidate sits across from an evaluator holding a rubric. STAR format: Situation, Task, Action, Result. Thirty seconds per answer. The evaluator checks boxes. Did the candidate mention a framework? RICE, RACI, OKRs? Did they cite the right acronyms in the right sequence? Did they tell a story with the expected arc—challenge, intervention, measurable outcome? The ritual has nothing to do with whether this person can lead. It measures whether they can produce the expected signal on demand. Compliance, scored as competence.

The rubric isn't evil. It exists because organizations must make hiring decisions at scale, and scale requires compression. You cannot evaluate a thousand candidates through deep conversation. You need a filter. The filter must be consistent, defensible, auditable. So you build a rubric. The rubric defines what leadership looks like. And what leadership looks like becomes what leadership is.

Here is the physics of the problem:

Excellence requires variance. The exceptional sits in the tails of the distribution, by definition. A leader who sees what others miss, who synthesizes across domains, who holds complexity without reducing it—that person deviates from the mean. Their value lies precisely in the deviation.

The Cage eliminates variance. Organizations formalize to scale. Formalization requires consistency. Consistency requires compression. Compression shaves the tails. What cannot be measured cannot be valued. What cannot be valued cannot be rewarded. What cannot be rewarded does not survive.

Therefore the Cage eliminates excellence.

The syllogism describes mechanism, not metaphor.

Organizations do not formalize because their leaders are cowards or their cultures are weak. They formalize because coordination at scale requires legibility, and legibility requires frames. A frame is a way of seeing that is also a way of not seeing. Metrics define what matters. What metrics miss becomes invisible. Optimization within the frame deepens the blindness. The organization gets better and better at the wrong things.

The compression begins before you walk through the door. The job posting encodes a frame: required skills, years of experience, industry background. The résumé screen applies the frame. The phone screen applies the frame. The interview panel applies the frame. At each stage, variance is eliminated. What remains is what fits the template. This is efficient. It is also how organizations ensure they never hire the person who would have changed everything.

The frame defends itself: challenges to the rubric appear, from within the rubric, as failures to meet it. The candidate who gives unexpected answers is marked as unprepared. The leader who rejects the acronym catechism is marked as unsophisticated. The person who treats humans as humans is marked as soft. From inside, the exclusion looks like quality control.

This is why reforms fail. Each generation discovers the problem—bureaucracy stifles innovation; process replaces judgment; metrics miss what matters—and implements solutions. Training programs. Culture initiatives. New frameworks to replace old frameworks. The solutions work temporarily. Then they decay. The pressure that created the original formalization remains unchanged. The new solution is absorbed into the formal system. Variance compresses again. The cycle repeats because the cycle is the system.

The mechanism intensifies at scale for reasons that are structural, even legal. Public companies operate under fiduciary duty. Directors must demonstrate prudent decision-making. Demonstrable prudence requires documentation: alternatives considered, experts consulted, metrics cited, formal approvals recorded. Decisions that cannot be documented cannot be defended. Decisions that contradict documented analysis invite liability.

This creates a rational calculus. A mediocre choice supported by thick documentation survives legal challenge. A superior choice lacking formal justification invites scrutiny. When outcomes are uncertain, optimize for defensibility over effectiveness. The incentive is unambiguous. Directors converge on documentable decisions regardless of which decisions might actually serve shareholders. This is adaptation to the legal environment, not failure of character.

The law did not intend this outcome. Courts cannot judge whether a strategic bet was correct—it would have required knowing counterfactuals and future states. They can only assess whether a decision was reasonable given available information. "Reasonable" becomes an evidentiary standard satisfied through formalization.

The legal system chose to prevent recklessness. The cost is reduced variance. The cost is the systematic elimination of the undocumentable insight, of judgment calls, of pattern recognition that cannot cite its sources.

The cost is excellence.

The Cage guards its own entrance. The people who satisfy the rubric get hired. Those people build organizations. Those organizations create hiring processes. Those processes generate rubrics. The rubric reproduces itself through selection before you ever see the inside.

The irony is precise. The process that eliminates the variance is correct on its own terms. The candidate who refuses the catechism would also refuse the internal rituals. They would not fire a good engineer to make the curve fit. They would not package accomplishments in consumable formats. They would not fight the right way, meaning the way the frame recognizes as fighting.

The rubric predicts, accurately, that this person will not perpetuate the rubric. It calls that prediction failure. The Cage protects itself by selecting for those who will maintain it. The variance it eliminates doesn't disappear. It goes elsewhere—starts companies and builds things the Cage will eventually acquire once someone else has absorbed the risk. It succeeds in terms the frame cannot measure and therefore cannot see.

Every calibration system that forces a curve kills high performers to make the distribution fit. Every evaluation that demands quantifiable outcomes erases the preventive work that produced "nothing happened." Every process that requires comparable precedent punishes the first mover. Every approval chain that demands consensus selects for ideas weak enough to threaten no one. These are not failures of execution. They are the system working as designed.

The person who can recite STAR format in thirty-second increments demonstrates mastery of a skill: performing for rubrics. The person who pauses to think, who asks clarifying questions, who refuses to compress a decade of judgment into a rehearsed anecdote—that person demonstrates a different skill. The rubric cannot distinguish between them. The rubric doesn't know the difference exists.

As though people aren't people.

You can replace the leadership. You can rewrite the rubric. The Cage remains.

The Cage has no villain. It has a law.

The law is this: formalization enables scale, and scale requires formalization. The benefits are real—coordination, accountability, defensibility. The costs are real—variance compression, blind spots, systematic elimination of what cannot be measured. The trade-off cannot be eliminated through better design or stronger culture. It can only be recognized and managed.

Recognition is the beginning. An organization that understands the physics can choose which incompleteness it will tolerate. It can build structures that protect variance instead of eliminating it. It can create spaces where judgment survives long enough to prove itself. It can treat the frame as a tool rather than a truth.

The Cage is constant, like gravity. You do not escape it. You engineer within it.

The question is never whether your organization has a Cage. Every organization at scale has a Cage. The question is whether anything counterweights it—whether some adaptation exists that preserves the variance excellence requires.

That adaptation is the Mirror.

Part IV

The Mirror

Engineering Within the Cage

The Mirror

I run an exercise with every team I lead. We talk about strengths and weaknesses, but not in the usual way—not the tired taxonomy of what you're good at versus what you struggle with. That framing belongs to performance reviews, and performance reviews flatten people into shapes that fit boxes.

I ask something different. I ask what energizes you, what makes time disappear, what you'd volunteer for if no one was watching. And I ask what drains you—the tasks you might execute flawlessly but dread, the work you procrastinate and avoid, the responsibilities that leave you emptied even when you succeed.

People hesitate. Everyone has been trained to hide this truth. The work you love feels selfish to admit; surely others want it too, and claiming it seems greedy. The work you hate feels shameful to reveal; surely it reflects some deficiency, some gap in professionalism or grit. We assume what drains us drains everyone. We assume what excites us excites everyone. We don't want to take the work we like because it feels like taking candy. We don't want to ask for help with work we hate because it feels like imposing.

So they write their lists cautiously. And with their permission, I share some responses with the team.

Then something happens.

Patterns emerge that no one could see from inside themselves. One person dreads planning but finds documentation meditative. Another loves planning but hates the reporting that follows. Someone avoids debugging like a root canal but lights up when testing reveals unexpected behavior. Someone else finds testing tedious but thrives when tracing a bug to its source. The task one person resents is the task another finds satisfying. The work that empties you fills someone else.

The room shifts. People laugh in recognition. Shoulders drop. The self-protection loosens.

The truth becomes visible: they were never meant to do this alone. They were meant to complete each other.

This is the Mirror.

The Mirror does not eliminate the frame. It reveals what the frame obscures. It does not replace judgment with process. It creates conditions where judgment can operate. It does not demand uniformity. It protects variance—the raw material of excellence that the Cage systematically eliminates.

The Cage says: do the task. Fit the rubric. Satisfy the metric. The Mirror says: ensure the task is done—by the person for whom it is fuel, not friction. The Cage compresses people into shapes that fit boxes. The Mirror orchestrates shapes that fit each other.

The exercise works because it makes complementarity visible. Before, each person saw only their own energy map: what they loved, what they dreaded, what they assumed was universal. After, they see the team as a system of interlocking differences. The documentation someone avoids is the documentation someone else finds calming. The planning someone dreads is the planning someone else needs in order to think clearly. What looked like individual weakness becomes collective strength, but only if someone arranges the pieces.

That visibility is the Mirror's function. The Cage operates through compression: reducing people to comparable units, measuring what can be measured, optimizing what can be optimized. The Mirror operates through revelation: showing the structure that compression hides, making legible what metrics miss, letting people see each other as complements rather than competitors.

The exercise scales.

A team that understands its energy map can self-organize around it. Tasks flow toward the people they energize. Collaboration replaces silent resentment. The work gets done better because the people doing it are not fighting their own depletion.

But organizations cannot run exercises with ten thousand employees. The insight must be embedded in structure—governance that protects variance instead of eliminating it, systems that formalize the recognition of what cannot be formalized.

This is where trust architectures emerge. The apprenticeship that transmits judgment through supervised practice because judgment cannot be codified into procedure. The red team chartered to challenge strategic assumptions because normal governance creates blind spots. The operational role granted explicit authority to deviate from procedure when conditions require, because procedures assume conditions that do not always hold. The innovation space protected from parent metrics because parent metrics would reject precisely what the space must explore.

Each of these structures does at organizational scale what the exercise does at team scale: it makes visible what the frame obscures, protects what the frame would eliminate, preserves the variance that excellence requires.

The structures share a common logic. They document that formal systems are incomplete. They create bounded space for judgment to operate. They protect that space from absorption back into the formal frame. Documentation proves to boards and regulators that variance is managed, not reckless. Boundaries ensure that experimentation has limits. Protection ensures that the mechanism survives long enough to matter.

Trust architectures decay. This is their nature.

The formal system exerts gravitational pull toward compliance, toward documented certainty, toward the elimination of variance that cannot be justified through approved metrics. Red teams that must seek approval before publishing findings lose the independence that made them valuable. Innovation units evaluated by parent metrics lose capacity to pursue opportunities those metrics would reject. Apprenticeships that assess only explicit skills lose the judgment transmission that was their purpose.

The frame absorbs what was meant to challenge it. The Mirror clouds. The organization maintains the form while losing the function.

Protection requires constant defense: governance independence so the mechanism reports outside normal approval chains; metric independence so evaluation criteria differ from parent measures; authority independence so decisions do not require validation through the frame. Without all three, the formal system gradually converts contradiction to compliance. The antibodies win. The variance compresses. The pattern disappears.

This is why you cannot copy another organization's culture. The visible structures can be replicated. The policies can be documented. But without the protection—without commitment at the highest level that these mechanisms serve essential functions and that erosion of their independence represents failure—the transplanted structures decay on contact with the host organization's logic.

The Mirror does not promise escape.

The Cage remains. Formalization is necessary for coordination. Legal requirements mandate fully documented process. Scale requires legibility. These constraints do not disappear because you recognize them. Even organizations that see their incompleteness still face the tension between demonstrated soundness and external perspective, between coordination and adaptation, between scale and variance. The Cage is gravity, inevitable and unyielding. Just as flight requires constant effort to escape it, so too does the Mirror exact its toll on those who hold it.

What changes is awareness. Unconscious drift toward formalization becomes conscious choice. The organization sees its walls and decides which to accept and which to challenge. It knows its metrics miss dimensions and chooses which dimensions to protect. It understands its procedures will prove insufficient and creates roles authorized to deviate when insufficiency appears.

A team that has done the exercise sees itself differently. They know that the person across the table dreads what they love and loves what they dread. They know that asking for help is trading, not burdening. They know that the system works because differences interlock.

That knowledge changes behavior. People volunteer for work that energizes them without guilt. People hand off work that drains them without shame. The team becomes more than the sum of its parts because the parts are no longer hiding from each other.

The Mirror makes this possible by changing what people can see. The tasks are the same. The people are the same. What shifts is visibility: the hidden structure of complementarity, revealed.

I cannot give you a Mirror. I can only describe what one looks like when it works.

A leader who asks the questions that remove fear rather than impose compliance. A structure that protects variance rather than eliminating it. A governance architecture that documents incompleteness rather than claiming sufficiency. A team that sees itself as interlocking differences rather than interchangeable units.

The Cage is constant, like gravity. You do not escape it. You engineer within it.

The Mirror is what lets you see where engineering is possible. It shows you the walls, the gaps, the places where judgment must substitute for procedure and variance must be protected from compression. It does not tell you what to do. It shows you where you are.

And seeing where you are—clearly, without the comforting illusion that the frame is complete—is the first condition of choosing where to go.

The Stakes

By now, you have seen the proof. Excellence is variance. The Cage eliminates variance. Therefore, the Cage eliminates excellence.

The syllogism is complete. What remains is understanding what it costs.

Excellence is not evenly distributed. It clusters in outliers—the engineer whose code prevents disasters that never appear in any metric, the translator whose synthesis enables seventeen teams while producing no artifacts of her own, the Janitor who knows the building better than the architects who designed it. These people exist. They are already on your payroll. And the cage is grinding them down or pushing them out, because the formal system has no way to see what they do.

To know whether an outlier is brilliant or broken, you must let them operate. You must give them variance. You must take the risk of being wrong. But variance is exactly what the Cage eliminates. Fiduciary duty demands defensibility. Defensibility demands conformity. Conformity demands sameness. And sameness means you never get the data that would tell you who was exceptional.

The manager who could see the outlier's value cannot act on it. Acting is indefensible. "I promoted someone the metrics said was underperforming because I perceived something I cannot prove" is a career-ending sentence. So the outlier leaves or stops trying. The metrics stay green. The capability drains away. The people who could have saved you learn the only way to be safe is to stop caring.

The traps are not independent; they stack. Every path to knowing requires risk the Cage will not tolerate. Scale says you cannot know without proximity—but proximity does not scale. Context says you cannot know without nuance—but nuance cannot survive compression. Legibility says you cannot know without seeing the invisible—but defending what you cannot prove is dangerous. Law says you cannot know without variance—because discovering truth requires trying things that might fail—but variance is indefensible under fiduciary review.

The Cage does not hate excellence. The Cage cannot see it. And what the Cage cannot see, the Cage cannot protect.

The Stance

The Mirror is the willingness to take the risk anyway—on behalf of something larger than yourself.

Not recklessness. Not rebellion. Intelligent risk-taking inside systems designed to forbid it. The capacity to see what the formal system cannot see, and to act on that perception despite the cost. This is what Mode B looks like from the inside: judgment taking responsibility where the formal system cannot.

What follows are demonstrations of intelligence operating inside the Cage. You will see how someone who perceives the geometry thinks, what they notice, where they apply pressure. The situations will be specific. Your context will be different. Your constraints will be different. Your edge will be your own. The understanding still transfers.

The goal is not to escape the Cage. The Cage is gravity. You do not beat gravity; you learn to design within it. The goal is to remain intelligent inside the constraint—to preserve variance where variance matters, to see what the metrics miss, to protect the outliers the system would grind down, to build structures that fail in new ways rather than calcifying into permanent blindness.

We will make better mistakes tomorrow. That is the only victory available. It must suffice.

CHAPTER 16

Navigating Hierarchy

The Tickets Company

I was hired as chief architect at a startup in San Francisco. They sold experiences—dinners, events, outings designed to get people into the world. The company was growing fast and accumulating the standard problems that come with speed. But these problems seemed unusually stubborn.

The site loaded slowly. Reports took forever. The SQL was intricate, full of joins that made simple questions expensive to answer. New features that should have been straightforward—like recurring Sunday brunch events—required surprising effort. Engineering had built a tool for cloning events, but it was flaky, so Business Operations developed a workaround: they edited existing events directly to change dates and prices. The checkout did not denormalize data, which meant these edits created integrity issues that rippled through reporting and inventory. Each problem felt discrete, but the pattern did not. Patch one, and another grew worse. The system pushed back.

After weeks of ruminating, I saw the connection. We called ourselves an events company. Everyone who worked there would have said so. But that framing was wrong. We were not an events company. We were a tickets company, and events were merely descriptions of the tickets we sold.

The entire data model had been built around events as the primary entity. Dates lived on events. Prices lived on events. Inventory was computed by joining events to purchases. Every query that asked "what's available this weekend" had to traverse that join. Every report had to reconstruct ticket-level data from event-level structures. Every new feature had to work around the mismatch between how the business thought and how the database was organized.

We made a few changes to the schema. Dates moved onto tickets. Prices moved onto tickets. Events became what they actually were: metadata describing a class of tickets, not the thing being sold. Suddenly, everything made sense. "What's available this weekend" became a simple filter. Reports ran fast. Recurring events no longer required special logic—you just added new ticket inventory for subsequent dates.

The problem had never been systems or tooling. It was perspective. Choose the wrong load-bearing variable, and every downstream system inherits the error.

The Load-Bearing Variable

Picasso made a series of eleven lithographs called The Bull. The first is a realistic rendering—muscle, hide, mass. Each subsequent print strips away detail. By the eleventh, what remains is a few lines: the essence of bull, reduced to its structural minimum. Nothing decorative survives. What remains is what cannot be removed without losing the thing itself.

This is distillation. Not simplification—distillation. Simplification removes complexity. Distillation finds the load-bearing structure and eliminates everything that is not load-bearing. Distillation is how the mind survives complexity. Architecture is the search for what must endure.

The tickets insight was distillation. Events felt essential because that was the language everyone used. But events were not load-bearing. They were a way of talking about tickets. The load-bearing variable was the ticket: the thing with a date, a price, a quantity, a purchase status. Once that became clear, the architecture could be rebuilt around what actually mattered.

Scale and Context are coupled traps. The Scale Trap says information degrades through layers—too many nodes in the chain, and signal becomes noise. The Context Trap says compression loses meaning—too much removed, and intent disappears. They share a root: finite human cognition forces us to compress reality into structures we can hold, and those structures shape what we can see.

The first move for navigating hierarchy is distillation. Know which variables are load-bearing. If you compress the wrong thing, you lose the signal. If you preserve the wrong thing, you carry weight that does not matter. The goal is lossless projection—compression where the lost data is immaterial.

Separation of Concerns

The second move is boundary. Boundaries without distillation are just walls. Berkshire Hathaway has roughly twenty-five people at corporate headquarters coordinating over sixty subsidiaries. General Electric, at its peak, ran thirteen divisions with four to five management layers each. These structures work because they reset the hierarchy at each boundary. You do not have a sixteen-layer org chart; you have a portfolio of seven-layer pyramids, each one healthy within its limits.

The architecture of Code mirrors the architecture of the organization because they share the same cognitive limit. A monolith where everything knows about everything else cannot scale—not because the code is bad, but because the cognitive load is unbounded. Every change requires understanding the whole. Every failure cascades. Every new feature has to navigate the entire dependency graph. When boundaries fail, cognition floods.

Clean boundaries create strategic ignorance. The checkout service does not need to know about marketing. The inventory system does not need to know about the recommendation engine. Each component can remain blissfully unaware of the others because the interface contract is clear: here is what I need, here is what I provide, everything else is not your concern.

This is not about control. It is about limiting what each part of the system must hold in mind. Hierarchy works when it enables ignorance—when it allows each layer to operate without carrying the cognitive load of every other layer. Distillation reveals the shape; boundaries preserve it.

The Gradient

Hierarchy is not ideology; it is geometry. The CEO carries maximum breadth and minimum depth—latest market shifts, current investor pressure, imminent regulatory risk, anticipated competitor moves, all held in mind at once. The engineer carries maximum depth and minimum breadth—a nuanced codebase, a complex toolchain, a detailed set of problems they know intimately. Between them is a gradient, each layer translating context from one coordinate system to another.

The Scale Trap is what happens when you stack too many layers: transmission loss between nodes. The Context Trap is what happens when you compress too hard: meaning lost within nodes. More layers, more transmission loss. Fewer layers, more cognitive overload. They trade off against each other. There is no point where both are optimal; there are only points where the trade is acceptable. The navigation stance is not "solve Scale" or "solve Context" but knowing where you are on the tradeoff curve and whether that is the right place for your situation.

The tickets company had the wrong abstraction, but it also had the wrong boundaries. Business Operations edited events directly because the tooling for creating new ones was broken. That boundary—between business intent and data integrity—had collapsed. Fixing the abstraction restored the boundary. Once tickets were first-class entities, the tools for managing them could be rebuilt properly, and Business Operations no longer needed to work around the system.

The answers shift as the business evolves. The seeing does not.

CHAPTER 17

Navigating Legibility

The Traffic Controller

The complexity of the internal platform grew with the company. Documentation lagged progress, as it always does. The map was fading faster than the territory changed. Second-order ignorance became a real problem: engineers did not know what they did not know, and thus could not ask the right questions. Institutional knowledge lived in oral tradition, passed through hallway conversations and Slack threads rather than wikis that no one updated.

One engineer held it together. He was constantly in Slack, fielding questions, directing people to the right channels, connecting them with the keepers of knowledge, ensuring that engineers who consumed the platform team's products were supported. He was well-liked, invariably optimistic, the kind of person who boosted morale just by being in the room. He had a knack for rolling up his sleeves and leading by example. "Well, let's do this. The sooner we start, the sooner we're done." When junior engineers got stuck, they went to him. He helped them think through problems rather than solving problems for them, which made each of them incrementally more productive. He was the force multiplier we always tell senior engineers they need to become.

But he did not do his tickets. The legible work was wanting.

He was placed on a performance improvement plan. I tried to argue that the engineering effort he saved the company collectively was more than enough to justify his salary. That we would be better off hiring another engineer to do those tickets and we would still be saving money. The math was obvious to anyone who looked at what he actually did rather than what the system measured.

It fell on deaf ears. The system could not abide being gifted a greater value when what it wanted was conformity. He was let go.

The Slack channels became instant chaos. No more traffic controller, no more direction, no more clarity. Engineers who had relied on him to navigate the platform's complexity were suddenly lost. Questions went unanswered or bounced between channels. The oral tradition that had kept institutional knowledge alive began to fragment. But the engineer that replaced him closed tickets like clockwork.

What the Metrics Missed

The Engineer's value was multiplicative. He did not produce output; he increased the output of everyone around him. The system measured individual contribution and saw underperformance. It could not see the field he was bending.

This is the Legibility Trap at human scale. Prevention manifests as absence—as problems that did not happen because he intercepted confusion before it became delay.

Multiplication distributes across others—the velocity he added showed up in their numbers, not his. Social glue resists quantification—you cannot put "made work enjoyable" on a dashboard. The metrics captured what was easy to measure and missed what mattered most.

I saw it because I watched how the team interacted with him. I heard stories of guidance and support. I noticed how his pragmatism and optimism shifted the energy in meetings. None of that projected onto the performance rubric. The rubric asked whether he completed his tickets. He had not. Case closed.

The Legibility Trap is not about bad metrics. The ticket count was accurate. The Engineer genuinely had not performed the work assigned to him. The trap is mistaking accuracy for completeness—assuming that because the measurement is correct, the measurement is sufficient. He was not invisible. He was illegible. The map was not lying; the map was simply missing the most important part of the territory.

Metrics as Inquiry

Metrics are streetlights. They illuminate what falls within their beam. The drunk looks for his keys under the streetlight not because that is where he dropped them, but because that is where he can see. Organizations do the same thing. They optimize what they can measure because measurement feels like control. The unmeasured drifts into shadow, and what lives in the shadow eventually dies.

The Engineer in the Slack channels was in the shadow. His work did not produce artifacts the system knew how to value. Everyone who worked with him knew what he did, but he was illegible to the formal process that decided who stayed and who left. Legibility determined his fate. Competence did not.

Teaching Perception

You cannot navigate legibility alone. The manager who sees what metrics miss will eventually leave or burn out, if no one else develops the same capacity. The goal is not to become the sole pair of eyes that can see the invisible. The goal is to cultivate perception in others.

I have a question I ask new engineers: "What is a buffer?" The question seems simple enough to have a quick answer, but it is rich enough to fill an afternoon. Some define it as memory set aside for temporary storage. But what about a buffer period between meetings? What does it mean to buff your car? What do all of these things have in common?

The answer I eventually help engineers arrive at: a buffer takes an erratic thing and makes it more consistent. You buffer burst data to get a consistent read rate. You schedule meetings with intervals between them in case some of them run long. You fill the irregularities in the paint to make a nice shine. When I got a dog, one engineer told me what to name her.

I once ran a book club on *Zen and the Art of Motorcycle Maintenance* for a team targeting a five-nines success metric. I could not tell them what quality was. I could not hand them a rubric that would produce that level of reliability. They needed to develop an intuition for quality that preceded measurement, a felt sense that something was right or wrong before any metric confirmed it. So we read Pirsig together over wine and dinner, and we argued about what quality meant, and slowly they began to perceive distinctions the dashboard could not capture.

The Costs of Seeing

But seeing carries its own burden. You will defend people the system wants to remove. You will allocate resources to work that the dashboard cannot justify. You will make decisions that look wrong to anyone examining only the legible evidence. And sometimes you will be wrong—the person you defended will turn out to be underperforming in ways you missed; the resource allocation will fail to pay off; the illegible work will prove less valuable than you believed.

The Engineer who held the platform together is gone. The Slack channels are chaos. The replacement does his tickets like clockwork. The system got what it measured. The organization lost what it needed.

CHAPTER 18

Navigating Law

The Letter and the Intent

The payment card industry has a security standard called PCI DSS (Payment Card Industry Data Security Standard). It governs how companies handle credit card data—encryption, access controls, audit trails. One of its requirements mandates strong cryptography: modern encryption protocols only, older vulnerable versions explicitly prohibited. Compliance is not optional. The auditors check.

Our API served thousands of legacy customers. Many of them had built integrations years ago, written by contractors who long since moved on, running on systems no one fully understood anymore. Forcing them all to upgrade their encryption would break those integrations. Some customers would manage. Others would churn. A few would litigate. On paper, the trade was simple: compliance versus churn. The business cost was real and quantifiable.

The literal path was clear: force the upgrade, break the integrations, accept the consequences. That was defensible. That was what the regulation said. That was the interpretation no auditor would question.

We chose a different path. We captured the encryption version and cipher strength for every connection. We checked credentials. For all new accounts, we forced the upgrade—no exceptions. For legacy accounts, we tracked who was still connecting with older protocols and made sure they understood the implications. They could continue operating, but they would not qualify for PCI compliance certification. The risk was known and accepted by them, not hidden from them.

Our team demonstrated that we met the intent of the rules. The purpose of the encryption requirement was to protect payment card data from interception. Legacy customers using older protocols were informed of the risk, excluded from certification, and monitored. New customers got the full protection. The attack surface the regulation was designed to shrink had shrunk. We did not reinterpret the standard in the dark; we constrained our interpretation to a clearly defined, well-understood edge case. It shipped.

The Absurd Literal

A sharp attorney from Legal was working on compliance with GDPR—the European General Data Protection Regulation that governs how companies collect and process personal information. She interpreted the law with precision: anything that could be tied to a person is personal data. If a log entry contains a timestamp and a user action, and you can connect that action to a person, the log entry is personal data. If a session token can be traced back to an authenticated user, the session token is personal data. If a device identifier correlates with a person's behavior, the identifier is personal data.

She was not wrong. The logic was sound. The regulation's text supported her reading. She was doing precisely what the system incentivized her to do: eliminate interpretive risk. But if you follow that interpretation to its conclusion, businesses cannot operate. Taken seriously, her reading made recording any action by any user a potential GDPR violation—and commerce runs on that record. Authentication exists to connect identity to access. Authorization exists to connect identity to permission. Every system that knows who you are becomes a liability. The literal reading did not just create a compliance burden; it made the normal operations of any company legally hazardous.

I pushed back. Our logs were fine. The abstractions were reasonable. The intent of GDPR was to protect individuals from having their personal data exploited without consent, not to halt all business operations across the globe. The law was written by humans who understood that companies would still need to function. The interpretation had to be practical enough to permit what the lawmakers clearly intended to permit.

The Chief Compliance Officer came in to mediate. The debate was real—both readings had merit. The literal interpretation was defensible in a courtroom. The practical interpretation was defensible in a boardroom. We landed on practical. The logs stayed. The business continued. The spirit of the regulation was honored even though the letter of it was interpreted in context.

Calibrated Risk

The Fiduciary Trap creates pressure toward the most conservative interpretation of every rule. Conservative is defensible. Conservative protects the decision-maker from blame. If you choose the most literal reading and something goes wrong, you can point to the regulation and say you followed it exactly. If you choose a practical reading and something goes wrong, you are exposed. You made a judgment call. Judgment calls can be questioned.

This pressure is real, and it is not irrational. The business judgment rule protects directors who can demonstrate informed, good-faith process. The safest way to demonstrate that is to follow the most explicit interpretation of every requirement. Deviation creates risk. The system selects for caution.

But the most cautious interpretation is often absurd. Regulations are written by humans operating under constraints. They cannot anticipate every situation. They use language that is necessarily general. The letter, applied mechanically, can produce absurdity. The spirit almost never endorses it. Following the letter, while violating the spirit, is not compliance; it is theatrical compliance that satisfies auditors, while missing the point.

Navigation requires understanding why the rule exists. What is the harm it is trying to prevent? What behavior is it trying to encourage? Once you understand the intent, you can find interpretations that serve the purpose without breaking the business. You are reading the law the way its authors would want it read if they could see your specific situation.

The risk is that you are wrong. Your reading of the intent might be self-serving. Your practical interpretation might be wishful thinking dressed up as valid reasoning. The auditor might disagree. The regulator might disagree. The judge might disagree. You are taking a position that could be challenged, and if you lose the challenge, you bear the consequences.

Playing With What You Can Lose

You do not bet the company on a novel legal interpretation. You bet something you can afford to lose.

In large organizations, you rarely have the authority to create protected space for judgment. The hierarchy exists precisely to prevent individuals from taking risks that could damage the whole. In many companies, your real freedom is how small you are willing to make the blast radius. You limit the scope of your deviation to something containable. If you are wrong, the damage is bounded. If you are right, you have a proof point that can justify broader adoption.

In small organizations, the calculation is different. There is no hierarchy to navigate, but there is also no buffer to absorb mistakes. You can move faster, but the consequences land directly on you. The question becomes: what is the worst that could happen, and can I survive it? If the answer is yes, you move. If the answer is no, you find a smaller scope where the answer becomes yes.

The PCI DSS situation was calibrated. We did not ignore the regulation. We did not expose payment card data to known vulnerabilities. We found an interpretation that served the intent, documented our reasoning, got explicit acknowledgment from the customers who would be affected, and limited our exposure to a population that understood and accepted the risk. If an auditor had challenged us, we had a defensible position. If they had rejected that position, we had a path to full compliance that we could execute. The risk was bounded.

The GDPR situation was calibrated differently. The stakes were higher—GDPR penalties are severe—but the absurdity of the literal interpretation was also clearer. No regulator could reasonably intend to shut down every company that maintains logs. The practical reading was not a stretch; it was the only reading that made sense.

The risk of being wrong was real, but the probability of enforcement against a reasonable interpretation was low. We documented our reasoning, maintained it consistently, and moved forward.

The Stance

Law is the amplifier. It takes the other traps—Scale, Context, Legibility—and crystallizes them into mandatory behavior. What the metrics say becomes what the auditor checks. What the hierarchy decides becomes what the board reviews. What the documentation shows becomes what the court examines. The pressure toward defensibility is structural, not cultural. You cannot escape it by having better values or smarter people.

But the law is also written by humans who understand that organizations need to function. The intent behind every regulation is compatible with business survival, because lawmakers know businesses need to survive. The letter of the law may produce absurdity when applied mechanically; the spirit of it almost never does. Navigation means reading the spirit clearly enough to find the interpretation that honors it, documenting your reasoning well enough to defend it, and limiting your scope carefully enough to survive being wrong.

The law is a tool for stability, not a suicide pact. When the text demands something inhuman, the text is almost always being misread.

CHAPTER 19

Where Intelligence Breaks

The Other Outlier

Everything in the previous chapters assumes you are right. You saw what the metrics missed. You read the intent behind the letter of the law. You found the load-bearing abstraction. You drew the clean boundary. You took the calibrated risk, and the risk paid off.

But sometimes you are wrong.

The engineer you defended turns out to be exactly what the metrics said: underperforming. The practical interpretation you championed gets rejected by the regulator. The abstraction you distilled is not load-bearing after all; it is decorative, and you built a system around something that does not matter. The boundary you drew creates strategic ignorance in the wrong place, and failures cascade because no one knew what they needed to know.

The Gaussian Graveyard Revisited

The Legibility Trap creates a graveyard at both tails of the distribution. Metrics cannot distinguish the brilliant from the broken; both look like outliers. The engineer who seems unproductive might be the force multiplier holding the platform together. Or they might be exactly what they appear: someone who does not do their work. The rubric cannot tell you which. Neither can intuition, not with certainty.

When you defend the outlier against the system, you are betting. You are betting that your perception is more accurate than the metric. Sometimes that bet wins. Sometimes it loses. The traffic controller I described earlier was real—his departure created chaos, and the replacement who did his tickets like clockwork could not fill the gap he left. But I have also defended people who turned out to be precisely what the performance review said they were, and it took longer than it should have for me to admit it. I saw potential that was not there. I projected competence onto someone who had learned to seem competent without delivering. The metrics were right then, and I was wrong.

This is not a failure of the Mirror; it is the cost of using it. If you only act when certainty is available, you will never act, because certainty is never available. The choice is not between being right and being wrong. You choose to either make judgments under uncertainty or to let the system's default judgments stand.

The system's defaults are biased in predictable ways—they erase prevention, multiplication, craft. But the system's defaults are not always wrong. Sometimes the person the metrics want to remove should be removed. Sometimes the conservative interpretation is correct. Sometimes the literal reading is the right reading.

The Limits of Perception

Perception is a muscle, but muscles have limits. You can train yourself to see what metrics miss, to ask what the dashboard cannot show, to notice the multiplicative value that resists quantification. But training does not make you omniscient. It makes you better, not perfect.

The patterns you recognize are patterns you have seen before. When a situation matches a pattern, your perception sharpens. When a situation is genuinely novel, your pattern-matching fails. You see what you expect to see. You interpret ambiguous signals through the lens of prior experience, and sometimes that lens distorts rather than clarifies. The engineer who reminds you of a past force multiplier may not be one. The compliance situation that resembles a past success may have critical differences you are not noticing.

Humility is not optional equipment. It is load-bearing. The moment you believe your perception is reliable enough to override the system without doubt, you have become dangerous. Not because the system is trustworthy—it is not—but because unchecked confidence in your own judgment is how smart people make catastrophic mistakes.

The Mirror requires doubt. It requires the constant question: what if I am wrong? If you never ask that question, you are not using the Mirror. You are using yourself.

The Cost of Being Wrong

When you defend someone the system wants to remove, and you are wrong, the cost falls on the team. They carry a colleague who is not contributing. They cover gaps that should not exist. They watch resources flow to someone who does not deserve them, while their own contributions go under-recognized. Your misjudgment becomes their burden.

When you distill to the wrong abstraction or draw the wrong boundary, the cost falls on the system. Failures cascade. Dependencies break in unexpected ways. The architecture you built with confidence becomes technical debt that someone else must pay down.

When you choose a practical interpretation over a literal one, and you are wrong, the cost falls on the organization. The regulator disagrees. The audit fails. The penalty lands. Your judgment call becomes a line item in a legal settlement or a case study in a compliance training. And sometimes you get fired for it.

The Mirror does not eliminate these costs. It trades one set of risks for another.

The system's defaults create predictable damage: excellence erased, outliers ground down, capability drained away invisibly. The system's mistakes are invisible, continuous, and compounding.

Your judgments may create unpredictable damage: specific mistakes, particular failures, costs that land on identifiable people and projects. Your mistakes are visible, episodic, and recoverable.

The predictable damage is diffuse and deniable. The unpredictable damage has your name on it.

This asymmetry is why most people do not use the Mirror. Seen from a career perspective, letting the system be wrong is often safer than risking being wrong yourself. The system's failures are no one's fault. Your failures are yours. It is safer to let the metrics decide, to follow the literal reading, to accept the conservative interpretation. When the damage comes—and it always comes—you can point to the process and say you followed it. The cover is institutional. The blame is distributed. No one is accountable because everyone is compliant.

The Mirror offers no such cover. When you see what others do not see and act on that perception, you own the outcome. If you are right, you may not get credit; the success will look like luck or like the system working as intended. If you are wrong, you will get blamed; the failure will be traced to your judgment, your deviation, your choice to override what the metrics said.

The outlier you protected was not brilliant. The outlier was broken. And because you argued for them, some of that brokenness is now yours.

Acting Anyway

This is not an argument against using the Mirror. It is an argument for using it with open eyes.

You will be wrong. Not occasionally—regularly. Your perception will fail. Your judgment will err. The outlier you protect will sometimes be broken. The interpretation you champion will sometimes be rejected. The abstraction you distill will sometimes be decorative. The cost of these mistakes will fall on people and systems you care about, and the blame will fall on you.

And you should act anyway.

Not because you are confident. Not because your track record is perfect. Not because you have some special insight that others lack. You should act because the alternative is worse.

The system, left to its defaults, will grind down excellence with mechanical certainty. It will erase prevention, punish multiplication, and select for the mediocre over the exceptional. It will do this not occasionally but constantly, not through malice but through structure. The damage is invisible, cumulative, and devastating.

Your mistakes are visible, episodic, and recoverable. When you defend the wrong person, you can correct course. When your interpretation fails, you can revert to the stricter reading. When your abstraction breaks, you can rebuild. The damage is real, but it is bounded. The system's damage is unbounded because no one is watching for it, no one is accountable for it, and no one is trying to stop it.

The Mirror is not about being right. It is about being willing to be wrong in service of something the system cannot protect. You take responsibility for outcomes the system would disclaim. You absorb blame the system would diffuse. You own mistakes the system would anonymize. This is the cost of seeing. It is not optional. It is not avoidable. It is the price of admission.

The Discipline of Doubt

Use the Mirror, but do not trust it blindly. Check your perception against other perspectives. Find people who see differently and listen to what they see. When your judgment conflicts with the metrics, ask seriously whether the metrics might be right. When your interpretation conflicts with the literal reading, ask seriously whether the lawmakers meant what they wrote. When your sense of someone's value conflicts with the rubric, ask seriously whether you are projecting.

This is the discipline of doubt. It does not weaken the Mirror; it strengthens it. Confidence without doubt is brittle. It breaks catastrophically when reality contradicts expectation. Confidence with doubt is resilient. It bends, updates, incorporates new information. The strongest conviction is the one that has survived serious challenge. The most reliable perception is the one that has been tested against alternatives.

We Will Make Better Mistakes Tomorrow

The Mirror does not promise success. It promises a different kind of failure—visible, owned, recoverable. It promises that when you are wrong, you will know it, because the consequences will be yours to face. It promises that when you are right, something will be preserved that would otherwise have been lost.

This is not a comfortable promise. It offers no guarantee, no protection, no institutional cover. It asks you to see what the system cannot see, to act on that perception despite uncertainty, and to accept responsibility for outcomes you cannot control. It asks you to be wrong, repeatedly, in public, with your name attached.

And it asks you to do this because the alternative— letting the system decide, following the metrics, accepting the defaults—is a slower and more certain kind of failure. The Cage does not make mistakes. It grinds. It erases. It selects. And it does so with no one accountable, no one responsible, no one watching.

We will make better mistakes tomorrow. That is the only victory available. But it is enough.

CHAPTER 20

The Proof in Uniform

The Paradox

The United States Army is one of the most successful large-scale organizations in human history. It has operated continuously for nearly 250 years across every climate, culture, and form of warfare. It has absorbed technologies from muskets to nuclear weapons, adversaries from British regulars to networked insurgents, missions from continental defense to humanitarian relief. It has survived catastrophic defeats, political interference, radical restructuring, and the chronic underfunding that follows every war. Through all of it, the institution has maintained coherence. It fights. It adapts. It endures.

The Army is also the quintessential Cage. It is a gargantuan Weberian bureaucracy governed by an intricate lattice of regulations, field manuals, and standing orders designed to standardize every conceivable aspect of existence (Weber 1978). UCMJ, the Uniform Code of Military Justice, makes deviation a crime. The hierarchy is absolute. The chain of command is law. Every process is documented. Every decision has a regulation. Every soldier knows, or should know, exactly what is expected of them at all times. The formal system posits that if every soldier simply follows the regulations, the machine will function with predictable efficiency.

Any veteran of the service knows this to be a fiction.

Beneath the polished veneer of the chain of command lies a churning, murky, and vital shadow system—a parallel structure of governance driven by oral tradition, informal networks, and sanctioned deviation. This shadow system is not a corruption of the Army. It is the very thing that allows the Army to function. The formal hierarchy provides legitimacy and resources; the informal network provides the adaptability and practical wisdom required to survive the friction of the real world. The Army operates two systems simultaneously, and neither can exist without the other.

This is not an accident. It is not a cultural artifact that persists despite leadership's best efforts to eliminate it. It is a deliberate institutional design, refined over centuries under conditions where failure means death. The Army proves that the Cage and the Mirror can coexist at scale— that you can have strict hierarchy and fluid adaptation, absolute regulations and pragmatic improvisation, formal accountability and informal effectiveness. You just have to admit that the formal system is incomplete, and then build the informal system with the same seriousness you bring to everything else.

The Architecture

The Non-Commissioned Officer (NCO) corps is not a rank structure. It is an institution within the institution—a parallel hierarchy designed specifically to hold the knowledge that doctrine cannot contain.

The formal Army has two tracks: officers and the enlisted. Officers hold commissions, exercise command authority, and bear legal responsibility for their units. They rotate through assignments every twelve to twenty-four months, building breadth across the organization. Enlisted soldiers—and the non-commissioned officers who lead them—stay. A First Sergeant may remain in the same battalion for a decade. A Command Sergeant Major may spend an entire career in a single branch. This longevity is not an accident of career management. It is the mechanism by which institutional memory survives.

The NCO corps maintains its own schools, its own promotion criteria, its own culture. The Sergeant Major Academy does not teach what West Point teaches. It transmits different knowledge: how to read a commander's intent beneath the words of an order, how to protect a unit from the friction of higher headquarters, how to keep soldiers alive when the doctrine fails. This knowledge cannot be written down because it changes with every situation. It lives in the judgment of experienced leaders who have seen enough to know what the manual leaves out.

The relationship between officer and NCO is formally hierarchical—the officer commands, the NCO advises—but functionally dialectical. The Second Lieutenant fresh from Officer Candidate School outranks the Platoon Sergeant with twenty years of service. The org chart says the Lieutenant gives orders. The reality is more complex. The Lieutenant has a map; the Sergeant knows the terrain. The Lieutenant learned the theory of navigation; the Sergeant knows where the unit actually is.

Army folklore is saturated with jokes about Lieutenants who cannot read maps, who get lost on land navigation courses, who invent inefficient new procedures because they are bored or ambitious. These jokes are not merely humor. They are cultural transmission, teaching the hierarchy of

247

practical wisdom over formal authority. The fresh officer who asserts rank over the Sergeant's tacit knowledge will get the unit killed. The Sergeant who undermines the officer's formal authority will collapse discipline. The successful unit operates in the gap between them.

This tension is not a bug to be eliminated. It is a design feature to be cultivated. The Lieutenant signs the papers and gives the orders. The Sergeant tells the Lieutenant which orders to give. The formal structure remains intact—legible, auditable, defensible—while the decision-making draws on the informal network. Both systems run simultaneously. Neither acknowledges the other directly. The Army functions because everyone learns to navigate the space between them.

The Support Channel

Formally, the Army has one chain of command. Informally, it operates a parallel structure called the NCO Support Channel. This channel allows NCOs to communicate laterally across the organization without involving officers. A First Sergeant in one company can resolve a dispute with a First Sergeant in another over a cup of coffee, bypassing the formal investigation that would involve Captains, Majors, and endless paperwork. The dispute gets handled. The mission continues. The bureaucracy never knows.

This lateral network functions like what organizational theorists call a permanent administrative layer—a professional cadre that maintains institutional continuity while the leadership rotates through. Officers come and go; NCOs remain. They know who holds the keys to the ammunition bunker, who can authorize a vehicle dispatch without paperwork, which administrative clerk can expedite a pay inquiry. This shadow grid is the true engine of daily operations. It cuts through bureaucratic silos because it is built on trust developed over years of shared service, not on the formal authorities that change with every new commander.

The most powerful tool of this shadow executive is the pocket veto. When an officer issues an order that violates the practical wisdom of the unit—an order that is dangerous, stupid, or impossible—the NCO does not openly refuse. That would be insubordination, punishable under the UCMJ. Instead, the NCO engages in creative delay, malicious compliance, or quiet workarounds that achieve the underlying intent while avoiding the specific stupidity. The order gets lost in translation. The situation changes before execution. The problem solves itself. The officer never knows their order was vetoed, and the unit survives to fight another day.

This is not corruption. It is shock absorption. The formal system assumes frictionless execution of rational orders by competent commanders. The real world delivers friction constantly, irrational orders occasionally, and incompetent commanders more often than anyone wants to admit. The pocket veto introduces elasticity into a rigid structure. It allows the organization to bend without breaking. Remove it—enforce every order with zero tolerance, eliminate all informal discretion—and the Army would suffer organizational stiffening and collapse under its own weight.

The Economy

Formal Army logistics are designed for efficiency and accountability. Requests flow up the chain. Approvals flow down. Supplies arrive in thirty days, properly documented, fully accounted. In garrison, this system works adequately. In combat, it fails.

War requires ammunition today. War requires vehicle parts when the depot is a thousand miles away and the roads are contested. War requires food when the supply convoy got ambushed and the formal system says the next delivery is scheduled for Tuesday. When the formal system fails, the unit faces a choice: follow the rules and die, or break the rules and survive. The informal economy exists because units keep choosing survival.

The scrounger is a universal military archetype, appearing wherever bureaucratic limits meet operational necessity. Roman centurions practiced *frumentatio*—foraging that bypassed the official governor's tax structures—because legions couldn't wait for requisitions from Rome. Napoleon institutionalized predatory logistics, permitting his Grande Armée to live off the land because speed mattered more than accounting. American advisors in Vietnam became "Czars of Scrounge," trading captured weapons and war souvenirs for barrier materials and ammunition because the formal supply chain could not reach their remote positions. The behavior is constant across centuries because the underlying dynamic is constant: formal systems optimize for accountability, and accountability is slower than necessity.

In the modern Army, "midnight requisition"—the acquisition of supplies through unofficial channels—is formally a crime. Property accountability is sacred; losing equipment can end a career. But acquiring a replacement to make the books balance is seen as resourcefulness, not theft. The supply sergeant who gives a neighboring unit extra batteries is not being charitable. They are purchasing an option on future assistance. When their own unit needs a vehicle part that is backordered for months, they cash in the favor. This lateral exchange system is faster and more reliable than the vertical requisition system because it runs on trust rather than process.

The formal logistics system is brittle. One disrupted node causes a cascade of failure. The informal network is anti-fragile—the more chaotic the environment, the richer the scrounger's opportunities become. Abandoned equipment, captured materiel, local purchases, creative repurposing—all of these expand when formal order breaks down. In a future war, when supply ships are sunk and air corridors are contested, the Army will survive on the scrounging capability of its NCOs.

The formal system cannot write a regulation that says "acquire supplies through unofficial channels when necessary" because that would destroy accountability. But it can cultivate a culture that celebrates resourcefulness, passes down stories of legendary scroungers, and implicitly signals that getting the job done matters more than getting the paperwork right.

The Transmission

The shadow system perpetuates through folklore. War stories, urban legends, barracks humor—these are not entertainment. They are curriculum.

When a senior NCO tells a war story to junior soldiers, they are conducting an informal case study. The stories focus on friction: the moment the radio broke, the map was wrong, the officer froze, the supply line failed. A manual says "call for fire." A war story says "when you call for fire, the battery might be eating lunch, so have a backup plan." This nuanced understanding of system failure is the primary value of oral tradition. It prepares the mind for the incompleteness of the formal system.

Army humor serves a similar function. Jokes about incompetent lieutenants teach new officers to respect NCO wisdom. The "Good Idea Fairy"—folklore's term for the bored officer who invents unnecessary procedures—warns against the dangers of technocratic overreach. "Skippy's List," a viral catalog of things one soldier was supposedly no longer allowed to do, represents what literary theorists call the carnivalesque: by mocking the rigidity of regulations with absurd specificity, soldiers vent the psychological pressure of living in a total institution, while validating the agency required to navigate it. The humor teaches that, while the rules are absolute, they are also often ridiculous, and surviving them requires wit as much as compliance.

Urban legends process the extremity of military life. The myth that Fred Rogers was a Marine sniper who wore sweaters to hide his tattoos reconciles the duality of the soldier—the quiet professional who is also a trained killer. Stories of informal justice, however dark, teach that the group has eyes and the group has consequences beyond what the UCMJ provides. These narratives transmit values the formal system cannot articulate: that loyalty to the brotherhood sometimes outweighs obedience to the chain of command, that the mission matters more than the manual, that survival requires judgment the regulations cannot supply.

The formal training system—TRADOC, the schoolhouses, the doctrine—produces soldiers who know *techne*. The informal transmission system—mentorship, folklore, observation—produces soldiers who possess *metis*. Both are necessary. Neither is sufficient alone.

The Strain

In 2006, the Army published FM 6–22, its keystone manual on leadership (Army 2006). The document is remarkable for what it almost admits.

Throughout its pages, formal doctrine strains against its own limits. The manual states: "Leaders are not always designated by position, rank, or authority. In many situations, it is appropriate for an individual to step forward and assume the role of leader." This is the chain of command confessing its own incompleteness—acknowledging that formal authority sometimes fails and informal leadership must emerge. It states: "Providing direction allows followers the freedom to modify plans and orders to adapt to changing circumstances." This is doctrine admitting that orders must sometimes be disobeyed, that rigid execution of commands from distant headquarters will produce failure in the face of local realities the commander cannot see.

The manual cannot quite say what it means. It cannot write "sometimes ignore the chain of command" or "sometimes the regulation is wrong." But it gestures at these truths constantly, because without them the formal system would break.

The 2006 manual was written during two simultaneous wars. Reality was pressing hard against the bars, and the strain shows on every page.

Later versions of the doctrine, written in peacetime, smooth over these admissions. The escape valves become less visible. The tension gets papered over with cleaner language about "mission command" and "disciplined initiative"—terms that acknowledge the need for decentralized judgment without quite admitting that this judgment sometimes requires violating orders. The informal system does not disappear; it cannot disappear, because the formal system cannot function without it. But it retreats into the shadows where doctrine cannot follow.

This is exactly what the framework predicts. Under pressure, the formal system reveals its dependence on the informal. When pressure eases, the formal system reasserts control and hides its reliance on what it cannot acknowledge. The shadow system remains. It always remains. But it speaks only in war stories, NCO wisdom, and jokes about Lieutenants with maps.

The Personal

I was in basic training, and my platoon was the first to go through the gas chamber. Given the Army's usual supply issues, not every soldier had a functioning gas mask. A drill sergeant told me to surrender mine because another soldier needed it. I complied. The exercise ended.

The rule was simple: anyone without a mask had to go back in to find theirs. This made sense as a punishment for carelessness—if you dropped your mask, you suffered the consequence, and you learned not to drop it again. Most soldiers without masks had been careless. I had not dropped my mask. I had surrendered it under orders. But the system had no category for "surrendered under orders." It had "has mask" and "does not have mask." I did not have a mask. I went back in.

The drill sergeants administering the exercise had neither the time nor the incentive to investigate each maskless soldier's story. Processing my individual case would have required intelligence and effort—understanding the context, verifying the order, making an exception. The formal system is not designed for exceptions. It is designed to process the general case efficiently. Apply the rule. Move on. The rule was not stupid. It was elegant: zero intelligence required to administer, self-selecting punishment for carelessness, minimal overhead. It worked in aggregate.

It just did not work for me, the edge case whose context did not fit the category. I breathed CS gas because the structure that punishes carelessness has no mechanism to recognize compliance.

There is a scene in a film where a soldier recovering in a hospital receives a bill for a jeep destroyed in combat. The audience sees absurdity—heartless bureaucracy tormenting a wounded man with paperwork for equipment lost in service to his country. The audience misses the elegance. The billing system accomplishes something remarkable: zero intelligence required to administer, minimal effort to implement, self-selecting filter for legitimate grievances. Bill everyone.

Soldiers who lost equipment in genuine combat will push back, provide documentation, and have the charges dismissed. Soldiers who lost equipment through negligence or theft will either pay or be caught when they contest. The system processes thousands of cases with a handful of clerks. Does it produce individual injustice? Yes. But the system was never optimized for individual experience. It was optimized for aggregate efficiency under constraint. Understanding that distinction is the first step toward navigating it.

This is what most people misunderstand about the Cage. It is not broken. It is not stupid. It is elegant, efficient, and effective at what it was designed to do. It just was not designed to be fair to you, the individual, the edge case, the person whose context does not fit the form. Fighting it by proving it is unfair accomplishes nothing, because the system was never trying to be fair.

The Bond

The formal system isolates. It demands individual compliance with universal rules. Each soldier follows orders, fills out forms, meets standards. The relationship is vertical: soldier to regulation, soldier to superior, soldier to institution. Compliance is lonely. You do it because you must.

The shadow system binds. When a squad leader tells his team they are going to ignore the uniform regulation today because they need to move fast, he is not just making a tactical decision. He is creating a conspiracy of competence. The soldiers who follow him are now complicit. They have shared a risk together. They have chosen the mission over the manual, and they have done it as a unit. This shared transgression creates loyalty the formal system cannot replicate.

The formal system asks for obedience. The shadow system asks for trust. When you break rules together to accomplish something that matters, you prove that you value the outcome—and each other—more than the bureaucracy. That proof becomes a bond stronger than any regulation can forge.

The formal system also overwhelms. It demands attention to everything: uniforms, forms, ammunition, safety, inspections, administrative deadlines, public relations. No human can hold all of it simultaneously. The cognitive load is impossible. Left alone with only the formal system, soldiers would shut down, paralyzed by infinite competing requirements.

The shadow system teaches triage. The NCO wisdom says: do not worry about the paint inspection; worry about the machine gun. This is not laziness. It is survival. The informal system tells you what to ignore so you can focus on what matters. It gives you permission to drop the ball on the trivial so you do not drop the ball on the vital. The formal system cannot say this—it cannot officially declare some regulations less important than others—but the shadow system can, and does, and must. Of course, this can be abused; some leaders hide laziness behind "focusing on what matters," and the difference is whether the mission and the people are actually better off. But without the triage that only informal wisdom can provide, the weight of the formal system would crush everyone beneath it.

The Proof

Military sociologists have circled this truth for decades without quite naming it. Janowitz (1960) documented the dual authority structure between officers and NCOs but framed it as professional sociology rather than institutional necessity. Scott (1998) described how legibility depends on local knowledge but treated informal systems as resistance to state power rather than designed complements to it. Stacey (1996) identified shadow systems as where organizational creativity happens but did not connect them to the formal system's structural incompleteness. What none of them made explicit—what rarely gets said clearly—is that large formal institutions must cultivate informal systems as a structural solution to the limits of formalization itself.

Gödel (1931) proved that any formal system rich enough to be useful contains truths it cannot prove from within. The Army is rich enough to fight wars. It contains truths it cannot write into doctrine: that regulations are sometimes wrong, that NCOs often know better than officers, that resourcefulness matters more than requisition forms, that the mission outweighs the manual, that loyalty to the people beside you sometimes supersedes obedience to the people above you. These truths cannot be formalized without destroying the formal system's coherence.

A regulation that says "ignore regulations when necessary" is not a regulation; it is an admission that the regulatory structure has limits. So the truths live elsewhere—in folklore, in oral tradition, in the NCO support channel, in the economy of scrounging, in the bond of shared transgression. They live in the space between what is written and what is understood.

The Army did not stumble into this architecture. It developed it over centuries, under conditions where getting it wrong means people die. The informal system is not a failure of discipline or a cultural accident or a problem to be solved by better regulations. It is the other half of the operating system. It is the part that holds the truths the formal part cannot contain. It is the Mirror built into the Cage.

If an organization with two million people and nuclear weapons can navigate this paradox—can maintain both the rigid accountability the mission requires and the fluid adaptation the battlefield demands—then so can you. The Army proves that these forces can coexist. You can have hierarchy and still have judgment. You can have process and still have wisdom. You can have compliance and still have effectiveness. You just have to stop pretending that the formal system is complete.

You have to admit that the regulations will never be sufficient, that the metrics will never capture everything that matters, that the doctrine will always lag behind reality. And then you have to build the other system—deliberately, carefully, with the same seriousness you bring to the formal one—and protect it from the Cage's constant pressure to eliminate what it cannot see.

The Army admits this, quietly, in the spaces between the words of its doctrine. It admits it in the jokes told about Lieutenants, in the war stories passed down through generations, in the lateral networks that keep units alive when the formal system fails. The question this book has been asking, from the first page to this one, is whether you will admit it too.

Gödel's Children

On the edge of the village there was always a small house with its door half open. Someone lived there, out of step with the village's clock—near enough to help, far enough to see. People brought hard problems to that threshold not because its resident was holier or cleverer, but because distance changes the angle of sight. The work was not authority. It was angle.

Ancient societies learned to formalize that role. They gave it names: the shaman who walked between sickness and spirit, the wise woman whose counsel balanced fear, the fool who could speak to the king because he owned nothing worth taking. Different titles, same geometry. The pattern is too persistent to be accident. Complex communities evolve a sanctioned outside.

Modern organizations prefer clean lines. We build systems that audit themselves, measure themselves, and certify themselves. The intent is good—legibility, repeatability, fairness—but the spike Gödel drove into the road in 1931 still lies there. Cold. Immovable. Completeness or consistency? You must choose. You cannot have both. You do not need the proof; you need the shape of it.

Once you see that shape, the corporate version stops being mysterious. A company is a formal system. It has rules, incentives, fiduciary duties, documented process, and metrics that claim to mirror reality. Those instruments are necessary; they are not sufficient. Process cannot prove that process is the problem. Metrics cannot show what metrics miss. Compliance cannot certify the moment when compliance destroys judgment. From inside, the frame always looks straight.

That is why the house at the edge persists. Successful systems require margin for external perspective. Close enough to know, far enough to understand. When that person says, "This is wrong," they are not projecting their values; they are exposing a truth unprovable from inside the system.

We have largely forgotten how to maintain that margin. We filter for agreement, optimize for defensibility, and sand away the edges that keep us alive. Originality returns as an external invoice: the consultant, the contrarian, the ungovernable principal engineer—vestigial shamans reintroduced under procurement. We keep them near enough to borrow their angle, far enough not to alter our lines.

To inhabit that role is to carry a paradox. You are asked to help and punished for how helping looks. What you contribute—an unaudited intuition, a joke that says what formal language cannot, a heresy that later becomes policy—arrives as error inside the rules. It fails the grammar check. So the person who offers it is tolerated, then resented, then called when the wheel slides off again. This is not bias; it is geometry. If you live there long enough, you start to wonder if you are the problem. You are not. The frame is.

Structures that endure learn to accept their own exceptions. Cultures that stay inventive keep the door cracked open; where it is closed, it reappears as attrition, shadow work, and black swans. Whether welcomed or not, the outside returns, because incompleteness is not a management opinion—it is emergent.

The old house remains. Someone still lives there. They complete the circle by contradiction, translating what the rules cannot say, holding up the Mirror that reveals the bars. They are not anomalies; they are proof. Every system rich enough to matter contains truths it cannot prove. Someone must stand just beyond the light and echo those truths back. The cage needs its children. Because truth, like pressure, always finds a seam.

Coda

You see it now.

The Cage was never hidden. It was always there—in the metrics that miss what matters, in the compression that strips meaning, in the law that crystallizes defensibility into mandatory behavior. You walked past it every day. You felt its friction without having words for the shape.

Now you have the words. The geometry is visible. The physics is clear.

What you build with that clarity is yours. The book cannot tell you. Your context is specific. Your constraints are local. Your scrap metal is whatever you find at hand.

The Cage is gravity. It will not stop pulling. The Mirror is not the escape. It is the decision to design anyway—to preserve what the system would erase, to see what the metrics miss, to act on perception despite the cost.

You will be wrong. The system will be more wrong.

That is the only math that matters.

Technical Notes

This appendix provides technical foundations for readers who want a deeper understanding of the empirical methods and key concepts used throughout the book. None of this is required to understand the argument. The book is intended to stand alone. These notes are for readers who want to verify claims, understand methodology, or explore technical details.

Measuring Language Compression

Two metrics are central to empirical analysis of language compression in strategic documents:

Lexical Diversity (LD) measures the breadth of vocabulary in a text. It is calculated as the ratio of unique words to total words:

$$LD = (\text{Unique Tokens}) / (\text{Total Tokens})$$

A text that uses many different words has high lexical diversity (LD approaching 0.20 or higher). A text that repeats the same words frequently has low lexical diversity (LD below 0.15). For context, conversational English typically shows LD around 0.18–0.22. Legal documents and regulatory filings typically show LD around 0.12–0.15.

The variance compression thesis predicts that strategic language in SEC filings should compress as organizations formalize. Empirically, S-1 filings (pre-IPO) show LD in the range of 0.16–0.19, while subsequent 10-K filings show LD declining to 0.13–0.15. This represents approximately

15–30% compression, depending on the company and time period.

Shannon Entropy (SE) measures information density and unpredictability in text (Shannon 1948). It is calculated using the formula:

$$SE = -\Sigma(p(w) \times \log_2(p(w)))$$

where p(w) is the probability of each word appearing in the text. High entropy means the text is unpredictable—many words appear with similar frequency, making it difficult to guess what word comes next. Low entropy means the text is predictable—a few words dominate, making the text more repetitive and formulaic.

For the benchmark used in this book: high-variance strategic texts (S-1 filings from founder-led companies) show SE scores of 11.5–12.5. Compressed post-IPO texts show SE declining to 10.5–11.0. The decline indicates that strategic language becomes more predictable and relies on a narrower set of repeated terms.

These metrics are not perfect. They measure linguistic variance, not strategic quality. A text can be high-variance and meaningless, or low-variance and precise. But when measured systematically across many organizations during formalization events (IPOs), the pattern is consistent: variance compresses. The compression is structural, not random.

A Note on Inference

This analysis compares the same company before and after IPO, measuring within-firm change over time. Patterns are then aggregated across companies to identify trends. The methodology does not compare CEOs across different organizations, does not treat documents from different contexts (earnings calls versus strategic filings) as equivalent, and controls for corpus size effects. The consistent direction of compression across cohorts suggests structural pressure, but readers should exercise caution when generalizing from these cross-sectional patterns to claims about any specific organization's trajectory.

The full empirical analysis, including company-by-company data, methodology details, and statistical tests, is available at cageandmirror.com.

Forced Ranking Error Rates

Error rates of 32% (random assignment) and 53% (realistic conditions with team quality variance) come from agent-based simulation modeling a technology company with 994 engineers distributed across 142 teams of 7 members each.

Simulation Methodology

Step 1: Talent Generation

The 994 individual talent values are drawn from a standard normal distribution $N(0,1)$. This creates a bell curve where approximately 68% of employees fall within one standard deviation of the mean, with tails representing exceptional and poor performers. This distribution matches the assumptions embedded in most HR systems and forced ranking implementations.

Step 2: Team Assignment

We implement two scenarios:
Random Assignment (Baseline): Engineers are randomly assigned to teams with no constraints. This represents the

best-case scenario for forced ranking—no hiring bias, no managerial quality differences, no favoritism. Team composition variance exists purely due to sampling variation.

Biased Assignment (Realistic): Team quality varies to simulate differential managerial capability. Implementation follows variance decomposition:

- Draw 142 team means from $N(0, 0.7)$
- For each team with mean μ_team, draw 7 members from $N(\mu\_team, 0.714)$
- Overall distribution maintains $N(0,1)$ by construction $(0.7^2 + 0.714^2 \approx 1)$

This clusters high performers in "strong" teams (good managers who attract and develop talent) and low performers in "weak" teams (poor managers). The parameter $\sigma\_team = 0.7$ represents moderate clustering—strong enough to be realistic, weak enough to be conservative.

Step 3: Ground Truth Identification

All 994 engineers are ranked by true talent globally. The true bottom 15% ($\approx$149 engineers) who should be terminated and true top 15% ($\approx$149 engineers) who should be promoted are identified. This ground truth is known to the simulation but not accessible to the forced ranking system.

Step 4: Forced Ranking Application

Within each team of 7 members:
- Rank members by talent
- Label bottom $\approx$15% (typically 1 per team) for termination → $\approx$142 total terminations
- Label top $\approx$15% (typically 1 per team) for promotion → $\approx$142 total promotions

Step 5: Classification Error Measurement

Compare forced ranking outcomes to ground truth:

Terminations:
- Correct: Fired AND in true global bottom 15%
- False Positive: Fired but NOT in true global bottom 15%
- False Negative: In true global bottom 15% but NOT fired

Promotions:
- Correct: Promoted AND in true global top 15%
- False Positive: Promoted but NOT in true global top 15%
- False Negative: In true global top 15% but NOT promoted

Error Rate = (False Positives) / (Total Labeled)

Results

Random Assignment (Best Case):
- Total labeled for termination: 142
- Correct terminations: 97 (68%)
- False positives (wrong people fired): 45 (32%)
- False negatives (deserving people not fired): 52

The promotion results mirror these numbers. Under perfect randomization with no bias, forced ranking produces **32% error** by construction. The variance in team composition—which cannot be eliminated—creates systematic misclassification.

Biased Assignment (Realistic Conditions):

- Total labeled for termination: 142
- Correct terminations: 66 (47%)
- False positives (wrong people fired): 76 (53%)
- False negatives (deserving people not fired): 83

Under realistic team quality variation, forced ranking's correct classification rate drops to 47%—**worse than random team assignment**, which achieves 68%. The **53% error rate** means more than half of terminations target capable employees trapped on strong teams, while more than half of promotions reward mediocre performers on weak teams.

Why The Errors Are Inevitable

The mechanism is straightforward. Consider two teams:

Strong Team (mean = +1.0σ): All 7 members are 60th-95th percentile globally. Forced ranking requires terminating one. That person might be 70th percentile—competent by any absolute standard—but is the "weakest" locally and gets fired.

Weak Team (mean = -1.0σ): All 7 members are in the 5th-40th percentile globally. Forced ranking requires promoting one. That person might be in the 25th percentile—underperforming 75% of the company—but is the "strongest" locally and gets promoted.

This is not a pathology. It is the necessary consequence of applying distributional requirements to non-representative samples. The system violates basic measurement principles: you cannot infer global properties from local observations when local contexts differ significantly and you have no mechanism to calibrate across contexts.

Key Assumptions (All Favor Forced Ranking)

Talent as unidimensional: We model talent as a single scalar. Real engineers have multidimensional capabilities, but forced ranking reduces these to a single comparative ranking. Our simplification mirrors the practice.

Known ground truth: We assume talent is perfectly observable. In reality, talent is only partially observable, introducing measurement error beyond the structural errors we demonstrate. Our results thus represent a **lower bound** on forced ranking's failure rate.

Static teams: Teams do not change composition within a simulation run. Real organizations have turnover, transfers, and growth that compound errors over time.

No gaming: Employees and managers do not strategically manipulate rankings. Real forced ranking creates incentives for politics, favoritism, and gaming. Our results exclude these behavioral distortions.

Normal distribution: We assume bell curve talent distribution, consistent with HR theory. Empirical research suggests performance in knowledge work follows power law distributions, which would make the problem worse (see Appendix B).

These simplifying assumptions all favor forced ranking. Real implementations perform worse than our simulations.

Sensitivity Analysis

We tested robustness by varying key parameters:
- **Team sizes:** 5, 6, 8, and 9 members per team
- **Talent distributions:** Lognormal and uniform in addition to normal
- **Cutoff percentages:** 10% and 20% in addition to 15%
- **Clustering strength:** σ_team from 0.3 to 1.0

The core finding holds across all variations. Random assignment produces 28–35% error. Biased assignment with realistic clustering produces 48–62% error. The pattern is consistent: forced ranking produces substantial errors that worsen with team quality variance—exactly as the frame problem predicts.

Implications

These error rates represent real human cost. In a 1,000-person organization under realistic conditions:

- 76 capable employees are wrongly terminated (career disruption, financial hardship)
- 83 underperformers are retained (reduced productivity, demoralization)
- 76 mediocre employees are wrongly promoted (occupy positions they're unqualified for)
- 83 deserving employees are denied promotion (under-compensated, likely to exit)

Every manager followed the process correctly. There is no procedural fix, no training intervention, no cultural shift that eliminates these errors. They are inherent to the system—the inevitable consequence of evaluating a global population using local frames.

The complete simulation code, parameters, sensitivity analyses, and power law extensions are available at github. com/jmcentire/forced_rank/ for readers who want to verify or extend the analysis.

Power Law
Distribution Effects

The analysis above assumes normal distribution of talent, consistent with HR theory's "bell curve" assumptions. However, empirical research (O'Boyle & Aguinis 2012) suggests performance in knowledge work follows power law distributions, where a small fraction of contributors produces disproportionate value.

We tested the simulation using Pareto distributions (shape parameter $\alpha = 3$, representing "10x engineer" phenomena) at varying clustering levels. The results reveal asymmetric failure:

Termination errors remain contained (~36–39%) because power law distributions have long lower tails—even weak teams contain genuinely poor performers. The "worst person on a weak team" is usually actually weak.

Promotion errors become catastrophic (61–80%) because exceptional performers cluster on strong teams. Under 95% clustering, the system promotes individuals averaging in the 56th percentile while claiming to identify the top 15%. Only 2 of ~10 true "1% performers" receive promotion; the rest are trapped on elite teams while mediocre "best of weak teams" advance instead.

This asymmetry creates a **ratchet effect** across multiple periods: wrong promotions compound as mediocre managers make hiring decisions, top talent observes that performance ≠ advancement and exits, and the organization systematically selects for employees who tolerate arbitrary evaluation. By year 6–10, the company achieves "statistical fairness"—error rates return to baseline—because the talent distribution has collapsed toward mediocrity.

The normal distribution results (32%/53%) presented above therefore represent **conservative lower bounds** that give forced ranking every benefit of the doubt. Real implementations under power law distributions can exceed 80% promotion error with multi-period talent degradation.

For Skeptics

This appendix is for readers who remain unconvinced. It provides three things: where to find the technical papers and code that support empirical claims, the specific conditions under which each major thesis would be falsified, and the strongest versions of the counter-argument from scholars who believe organizational dysfunction is fixable rather than structural. The framework is falsifiable. The evidence is public. The dissent is real. Readers who want to challenge the argument have everything they need to do so.

Where to Go Deeper

The full technical papers supporting empirical claims in this book—including complete methodology, datasets, simulation code, and extended case studies—are available at *cageandmirror.com*. These papers are written for academic and technical audiences. The book is intended to be accessible without them.

Readers interested in extending the framework, testing propositions in their own organizational contexts, or engaging with the mathematical and legal foundations will find the technical papers essential. Readers satisfied with the book's treatment of concepts and evidence can ignore the papers entirely.

On Falsifiability

A scientific claim is falsifiable if you can specify in advance what evidence would prove it wrong. The claims in this book are falsifiable:

The **Cage framework** would be falsified if organizations operating under high formalization and high fiduciary duty consistently maintained strategic variance, adapted rapidly to environmental change, and preserved capabilities that resist measurement—without building the kind of parallel structures the Mirror describes.

The **dysmemic pressure thesis** would be falsified if organizations with high preference divergence, low verification costs, and high transmission ease consistently maintained accurate internal information flow—or if interventions targeting "culture" without altering incentive structures, transmission channels, or verification mechanisms produced durable improvements in organizational epistemic quality.

The **forced ranking error claim** would be falsified if simulation under realistic conditions showed error rates below 20%, or if real-world organizations using forced ranking could demonstrate that their termination and promotion decisions correctly identified actual bottom and top performers at rates significantly better than random chance. The claim would also be falsified if organizations could eliminate the error through procedural refinements like calibration sessions, absolute standards, or hybrid approaches.

The **variance compression thesis** would be falsified if systematic analysis of pre-IPO and post-IPO strategic documents showed no consistent pattern of linguistic compression, or if the compression appeared randomly rather than correlating with formalization events.

The claims in this book are not rhetorical. They are testable propositions. The fact that they have not been falsified despite extensive evidence does not prove they are true in all contexts. It proves they describe real patterns that operate across many contexts. The book specifies boundary conditions where effects should be strong (public companies, regulated industries, dispersed ownership) versus weak (private companies, concentrated ownership, fast feedback loops).

Readers who want to test these claims in their own organizations, or who want access to the full datasets and simulation code, can find resources at cageandmirror.com.

On Deming and the Quality Tradition

Readers familiar with W. Edwards Deming (1986) may wonder whether this book rejects statistical quality thinking. It does not.

Deming understood that systems produce variation, that most variation is structural rather than individual, and that tampering with stable processes based on point-to-point comparisons makes things worse. His critique of management by numbers—ranking workers, setting quotas, demanding numerical goals without providing methods—anticipates much of this book's argument. The Cage framework builds on these insights.

The divergence is in scope. Deming's methods were forged in manufacturing, where processes have defined inputs, measurable outputs, and controllable parameters. Statistical process control works because the system can be observed, measured, and adjusted without fundamentally altering what is being measured. The Cage emerges when these methods migrate to knowledge work, strategic decision-making, and organizational governance—domains where the act of measuring changes what is measured, where the relevant variables resist quantification, and where the pursuit of metric stability destroys the variance that produces excellence.

Deming himself warned against this. His seventh point, "Institute leadership," distinguished supervision that helps people do better work from supervision that merely monitors output. The Cage is what happens when organizations forget the distinction.

Dissenting Voices

Readers who find the Cage framework too pessimistic should engage with the strongest versions of the counter-argument. These works represent the optimistic tradition at its most rigorous.

Organizational Culture and Leadership by Edgar Schein (5th edition, 2017) argues that leaders are "primary architects of culture" who can embed and reinforce cultural standards through deliberate intervention. Schein acknowledges that underlying assumptions are difficult to change, but maintains that leadership can overcome structural constraints. The Cage framework treats culture as downstream of structure; Schein treats structure as downstream of culture. Readers should evaluate which framing better explains their organizational experience.

Organization Change: Theory and Practice by W. Warner Burke (6th edition, 2023) provides the most comprehensive treatment of change management as systematic, achievable intervention. Burke's 12-factor model assumes that formal systems can capture organizational dynamics sufficiently to guide transformation. If the Cage framework is wrong about incompleteness, Burke's approach should work more often than it does. The 70% failure rate of change initiatives is either an execution problem (Burke's view) or evidence of structural constraints (this book's view).

Organization Theory and Design by Richard Daft (13th edition, 2021) represents the engineering paradigm at textbook scale. Daft treats organizational structure as a design variable to be optimized through rational analysis, with hierarchy as a tool rather than a constraint. This is the standard business school framing that the Cage framework explicitly rejects. Readers who find the rejection unconvincing should work through Daft's logic carefully.

High Output Management by Andrew Grove (1983) demonstrates what Mode B leadership looks like from the inside, though Grove would not have used that language. Grove's emphasis on leverage, one-on-ones, and management as craft provides practical wisdom for operating within constraints. The book assumes constraints can be navigated rather than eliminated, placing it closer to the Cage framework than the change management tradition, though Grove remains fundamentally optimistic about what good management can achieve.

Glossary

Algedonic Signal: Dedicated channel bypassing standard filters to transmit survival-critical alerts directly from frontline to policy level; from Beer's Viable System Model.

Babbling Equilibrium: Communication state where messages are statistically independent of truth; emerges when sender-receiver preference divergence exceeds threshold. From Crawford-Sobel strategic information transmission theory (Crawford and Sobel 1982).

Cage, The: The structural constraint emerging when fiduciary duty demands demonstrable soundness, scale requires formal systems, and reality refuses to compress without loss. The systematic consequence of necessary structures meeting mathematical and cognitive limits.

Channel Capacity: The maximum rate at which information can traverse a communication link without error; in organizations, the cognitive bandwidth of managers and communication channels.

Conservative Methodology: Estimation techniques that deliberately understate uncertain values using lower bounds, documented assumptions, and explicit confidence intervals. Not rhetorical hedging—what makes uncertain claims defensible under fiduciary scrutiny.

Context Trap: The structural schism where executives possess high-level context without local resolution, while frontline possesses high-fidelity local context without strategic coherence; resolved through hierarchical distillation.

Dysmemic Pressure: Selection force favoring cultural variants that increase individual payoff while decreasing collective adaptability; operates when internal fitness (career advancement, status maintenance) negatively correlates with external fitness (organizational adaptation, accurate information flow).

External Perspective: The structural requirement that no formal system can validate itself from within; requires outside view from parties who do not share internal frames or incentives.

Fiduciary Trap: Legal structure demanding demonstrable soundness that creates selection pressure toward formalization, amplifying organizational incompleteness into systematic bias toward what can be documented over what actually matters.

Frame: The collection of metrics, procedures, and documentation enabling organizational coordination; necessarily compresses reality and systematically preserves what fits categories, while erasing what does not.

Geometry: The specific pattern of what your formal systems can and cannot measure; determines what work gets erased and who pays the price in your particular organizational context.

Holacracy: A specific method of decentralized management that replaces top-down hierarchy with self-organizing teams governed by a formal constitution. It distributes authority to explicit roles rather than managers, attempting to replace the political structure of a firm with a transparent, rule-based operating system.

Legibility: The property of being visible to formal systems; work that produces artifacts, projects onto metrics, and fits standard categories is legible, while prevention, multiplication, and craft remain illegible.

Legibility Tax: Systematic disadvantage borne by people whose work resists formalization—prevention that manifests as absence of failures, multiplication across boundaries, and craft that defies quantification.

Mirror, The: Structures built deliberately within Cage constraints, using conservative methodology, external validation, and explicit acknowledgment of incompleteness to make invisible work legible to governance. Does not escape the Cage—operates within it.

Mission Command (Auftragstaktik): Military doctrine transmitting Intent (why and what) while withholding Instruction (how), enabling decentralized execution within strategic coherence.

Mode A: Organizational response pretending frames are complete; adds more metrics, process, and documentation when gaps appear. Optimizes for demonstrable soundness by claiming certainty exists. The maps thicken; the territory thins.

Mode B: Organizational response acknowledging frames are incomplete; builds parallel structures to capture what primary frames miss. Optimizes for demonstrable soundness by documenting sophisticated engagement with uncertainty rather than claiming it does not exist.

Schema Formation: Cognitive mechanism treating complex knowledge structures as single chunks in working memory; hierarchy functions as a distributed schema-building mechanism.

Shadow Price: Economic value of capabilities that do not appear in accounting systems until lost; theoretical value of constraints that only become visible when they bind.

Transmission Bias: Mechanisms by which cultural variants spread independent of truth value; includes content bias (simplicity wins), prestige bias (copy the successful), and conformity bias (copy the common).

Variance Compression: Measurable narrowing of strategic language, behavioral repertoire, or decision-making range occurring when organizations formalize; structural adaptation to legal and coordination requirements, not stylistic preference.

Variety Amplification: Downward expansion of low-variety strategic commands into high-variety tactical actions.

Variety Attenuation: Upward absorption of complexity by middle layers, filtering tactical noise before it reaches strategic level.

Bibliography

This bibliography provides formal citations for works referenced in the text. Readers seeking extended discussion of theoretical foundations should consult Appendix C: Related Research. Readers seeking methodology for empirical claims should consult Appendix A: Technical Notes.

Legal Cases

Brehm v. Eisner, 746 A.2d 244 (Del. 2000).
Chur v. Eighth Judicial District Court, 520 P.3d 310 (Nev. 2022).
Corwin v. KKR Financial Holdings LLC, 125 A.3d 304 (Del. 2015).
Gagliardi v. TriFoods International, Inc., 683 A.2d 1049 (Del. Ch. 1996).
In re Caremark International Inc. Derivative Litigation, 698 A.2d 959 (Del. Ch. 1996).
In re Citigroup Inc. Shareholder Derivative Litigation, 964 A.2d 106 (Del. Ch. 2009).
In re McDonald's Corporation Stockholder Derivative Litigation, C.A. No. 2021-0324-JTL (Del. Ch. 2023).

In re Walt Disney Co. Derivative Litigation, 906 A.2d 27
(Del. 2006).
Lyondell Chemical Co. v. Ryan, 970 A.2d 235
(Del. 2009).
Sample v. Morgan, 914 A.2d 647 (Del. Ch. 2007).
Smith v. Van Gorkom, 488 A.2d 858 (Del. 1985).
Tornetta v. Musk, C.A. No. 2018-0408-KSJM (Del. Ch.
Jan. 30, 2024).

Statutes and Regulatory Frameworks

Delaware General Corporation Law, Del. Code Ann. tit.
8, §101 (2025).
Delaware General Corporation Law § 102(b)(7) (Director
Exculpation Provision).
Sarbanes-Oxley Act of 2002, Pub. L. No. 107-204, 116
Stat. 745.
Texas Business Organizations Code § 21.419, as amended
by Senate Bill 29, 88th Texas Legislature (2023).

Mathematics, Information Theory, and Formal Systems

Gödel, Kurt. 1931. "Über formal unentscheidbare Sätze
der Principia Mathematica und verwandter Systeme
I" [On Formally Undecidable Propositions of
Principia Mathematica and Related Systems].
Monatshefte für Mathematik und Physik 38:
173–198.
Shannon, Claude E. 1948. "A Mathematical Theory
of Communication." *The Bell System Technical
Journal* 27: 379–423, 623–656.

Tishby, Naftali, Fernando C. Pereira, and William Bialek. 1999. "The Information Bottleneck Method." In *Proceedings of the 37th Annual Allerton Conference on Communication, Control, and Computing,* 368–377.

Measurement and Metrics

Campbell, Donald T. 1976. "Assessing the Impact of Planned Social Change." *Occasional Paper Series* 8. Dartmouth College, The Public Affairs Center.

Goodhart, Charles A. E. 1975. "Problems of Monetary Management: The U.K. Experience." In *Papers in Monetary Economics,* vol. 1. Reserve Bank of Australia.

Muller, Jerry Z. 2018. *The Tyranny of Metrics.* Princeton: Princeton University Press.

Cognitive Science and Information Processing

Miller, George A. 1956. "The Magical Number Seven, Plus or Minus Two: Some Limits on Our Capacity for Processing Information." *Psychological Review* 63, no. 2: 81–97.

Sweller, John. 1988. "Cognitive Load During Problem Solving: Effects on Learning." *Cognitive Science* 12, no. 2: 257–285.

Tversky, Amos, and Daniel Kahneman. 1971. "Belief in the Law of Small Numbers." *Psychological Bulletin* 76, no. 2: 105–110.

Cybernetics and Systems Theory

Ashby, W. Ross. 1956. *An Introduction to Cybernetics.*
London: Chapman & Hall.
Beer, Stafford. 1981. *Brain of the Firm.* 2nd ed.
Chichester: John Wiley & Sons.
Conway, Melvin E. 1967. "How Do Committees Invent?"
Datamation 14, no. 4: 28–31.
Meadows, Donella H. 2008. *Thinking in Systems: A
Primer.* Edited by Diana Wright. White River
Junction, VT: Chelsea Green Publishing.
Perrow, Charles. 1984. *Normal Accidents: Living with
High-Risk Technologies.* New York: Basic Books.

Organizational Theory and Behavioral Science

Argyris, Chris. 2004. *Reasons and Rationalizations: The
Limits to Organizational Knowledge.* Oxford:
Oxford University Press.
Argyris, Chris, and Donald A. Schön. 1978.
*Organizational Learning: A Theory of Action
Perspective.* Reading, MA: Addison-Wesley.
Burke, W. Warner. 2023. *Organization Development:
A Process of Learning and Changing.* 6th ed.
Thousand Oaks, CA: SAGE.
Cyert, Richard M., and James G. March. 1963. *A
Behavioral Theory of the Firm.* Englewood Cliffs,
NJ: Prentice-Hall.
Daft, Richard L. 2021. *Organization Theory and Design.*
13th ed. Boston: Cengage Learning.
Jackall, Robert. 1988. *Moral Mazes: The World of
Corporate Managers.* New York: Oxford
University Press.

March, James G. 1991. "Exploration and Exploitation in Organizational Learning." *Organization Science* 2, no. 1: 71–87.

March, James G., and Johan P. Olsen. 1975. "The Uncertainty of the Past: Organizational Learning Under Ambiguity." *European Journal of Political Research* 3: 147–171.

Schein, Edgar H. 2017. *Organizational Culture and Leadership*. 5th ed. Hoboken, NJ: Wiley.

Simon, Herbert A. 1947. *Administrative Behavior: A Study of Decision-Making Processes in Administrative Organizations*. New York: Macmillan.

Stacey, Ralph D. 1996. *Strategic Management and Organisational Dynamics*. 2nd ed. London: Pitman.

Weber, Max. 1978. *Economy and Society: An Outline of Interpretive Sociology*. Edited by Guenther Roth and Claus Wittich. Berkeley: University of California Press. First published 1922.

Scale, Hierarchy, and Organizational Structure

Bain & Company. 2010. "Streamlining Spans and Layers." Bain Brief.

Chandler, Alfred D. 1962. *Strategy and Structure: Chapters in the History of the Industrial Enterprise*. Cambridge, MA: MIT Press.

Davis, Ralph C. 1951. *The Fundamentals of Top Management*. New York: Harper & Brothers.

Freeman, Jo. 1972. "The Tyranny of Structurelessness." *The Second Wave* 2, no. 1.

Gordon, Cameron. 2022. "The Information Bottleneck Principle in Corporate Hierarchies." arXiv preprint arXiv:2210.14861.

Graicunas, V. A. 1933. "Relationship in Organization." *Bulletin of the International Management Institute* 7: 39–42.

Keren, Michael, and David Levhari. 1979. "The Optimum Span of Control in a Pure Hierarchy." *Management Science* 25, no. 11: 1162–1172.

Parkinson, C. Northcote. 1955. "Parkinson's Law." *The Economist*, November 19.

Performance Evaluation and Ranking Systems

Bradley, Ralph Allan, and Milton E. Terry. 1952. "Rank Analysis of Incomplete Block Designs: I. The Method of Paired Comparisons." *Biometrika* 39, no. 3/4: 324–345.

Elo, Arpad. 1978. *The Rating of Chessplayers, Past and Present*. New York: Arco.

Glickman, Mark E. 1999. "Parameter Estimation in Large Dynamic Paired Comparison Experiments." *Journal of the Royal Statistical Society: Series C (Applied Statistics)* 48, no. 3: 377–394.

Grote, Dick. 2005. *Forced Ranking: Making Performance Management Work*. Boston: Harvard Business School Press.

Herbrich, Ralf, Tom Minka, and Thore Graepel. 2007. "TrueSkill: A Bayesian Skill Rating System." In *Advances in Neural Information Processing Systems* 19. Cambridge, MA: MIT Press.

Luce, R. Duncan. 1959. *Individual Choice Behavior: A Theoretical Analysis*. New York: Wiley.

O'Boyle, Ernest, and Herman Aguinis. 2012. "The Best and the Rest: Revisiting the Norm of Normality of Individual Performance." *Personnel Psychology* 65, no. 1: 79–119.

Thurstone, L. L. 1927. "A Law of Comparative Judgment." *Psychological Review* 34, no. 4: 273–286.

Legibility, State Capacity, and Local Knowledge

Ostrom, Elinor. 1990. *Governing the Commons: The Evolution of Institutions for Collective Action.* Cambridge: Cambridge University Press.

Scott, James C. 1998. *Seeing Like a State: How Certain Schemes to Improve the Human Condition Have Failed.* New Haven: Yale University Press.

Military Sociology and High-Reliability Organizations

Army, U.S. 2006. FM 6-22: Army Leadership; Competent, Confident, and Agile. Washington, D.C.: Department of the Army.

Army, U.S.. 2019. *Mission Command: Command and Control of Army Forces.* Army Doctrine Publication 6-0. Washington, DC: Headquarters, Department of the Army.

Army, U.S. 2019. *Army Leadership and the Profession.* Army Doctrine Publication 6-22. Washington, DC: Headquarters, Department of the Army.

Janowitz, Morris. 1960. *The Professional Soldier: A Social and Political Portrait.* Glencoe, IL: Free Press.

McChrystal, Stanley, Tantum Collins, David Silverman, and Chris Fussell. 2015. *Team of Teams: New Rules of Engagement for a Complex World*. New York: Portfolio.

Vaughan, Diane. 1996. *The Challenger Launch Decision: Risky Technology, Culture, and Deviance at NASA*. Chicago: University of Chicago Press.

Weick, Karl E., and Kathleen M. Sutcliffe. 2007. *Managing the Unexpected: Resilient Performance in an Age of Uncertainty*. 2nd ed. San Francisco: Jossey-Bass.

Corporate Law Commentary

Bainbridge, Stephen M. 2004. "The Business Judgment Rule as Abstention Doctrine." *Vanderbilt Law Review* 57, no. 1: 83–130.

Kraakman, Reinier, John Armour, Paul Davies, Luca Enriques, Henry Hansmann, Gerard Hertig, Klaus Hopt, Hideki Kanda, and Edward Rock. 2009. *The Anatomy of Corporate Law: A Comparative and Functional Approach*. 2nd ed. Oxford: Oxford University Press.

Pinto, Arthur R., and Douglas M. Branson. 2009. *Understanding Corporate Law*. 3rd ed. Newark, NJ: LexisNexis.

Strine, Leo E., Jr. 2015. "The Dangers of Denial: The Need for a Clear-Eyed Understanding of the Power and Accountability Structure Established by the Delaware General Corporation Law." *Wake Forest Law Review* 50: 761–793.

Convergent Frameworks

Tomanek, Paweł. 2018. "The Tree, the Cage, and the Mirror: Cultural Reflexivity vs. Tradition and Rationalisation." *Societas/Communitas* 26, no. 2: 73–96.

Tomanek, Paweł. 2024–2025. "Epistemic Collapse in Scaled Organizations." Working paper.

Foundational Texts on Incompleteness

Goldstein, Rebecca. 2005. *Incompleteness: The Proof and Paradox of Kurt Gödel*. New York: W. W. Norton.

Hofstadter, Douglas R. 1979. *Gödel, Escher, Bach: An Eternal Golden Braid*. New York: Basic Books.

Nagel, Ernest, and James R. Newman. 2001. *Gödel's Proof*. Rev. ed. New York: New York University Press. First published 1958.

Antifragility and Variance

Taleb, Nassim Nicholas. 2012. *Antifragile: Things That Gain from Disorder*. New York: Random House.

Game Theory and Strategic Communication

Crawford, Vincent P., and Joel Sobel. 1982. "Strategic Information Transmission." *Econometrica* 50, no. 6: 1431–1451.

Prendergast, Canice. 1993. "A Theory of 'Yes Men.'" *American Economic Review* 83, no. 4: 757–770.

Cultural Evolution

Boyd, Robert, and Peter J. Richerson. 1985. *Culture and the Evolutionary Process*. Chicago: University of Chicago Press.

Supplementary Works

Bakhtin, Mikhail. 1968. *Rabelais and His World.* Translated by Hélène Iswolsky. Cambridge, MA: MIT Press.

Christensen, Clayton M. 1997. *The Innovator's Dilemma: When New Technologies Cause Great Firms to Fail.* Boston: Harvard Business School Press.

Deming, W. Edwards. 1986. *Out of the Crisis.* Cambridge, MA: MIT Press.

Feynman, Richard P.1988. *"What Do You Care What Other People Think?": Further Adventures of a Curious Character.* New York: W. W. Norton.

Grove, Andrew S. 1983. *High Output Management.* New York: Random House.

Lewis, Marianne W. 2000. "Exploring Paradox: Toward a More Comprehensive Guide." *Academy of Management Review* 25, no. 4: 760–776.

Page, Lawrence, Sergey Brin, Rajeev Motwani, and Terry Winograd. 1999. "The PageRank Citation Ranking: Bringing Order to the Web." Technical Report, Stanford InfoLab.

Pirsig, Robert M. 1974. *Zen and the Art of Motorcycle Maintenance: An Inquiry into Values.* New York: William Morrow.

Author's Supporting Research

The following papers provide extended methodology, simulation results, and detailed analysis supporting claims in this book. All are available at *cageandmirror.com*.

Core Theory

McEntire, Jeremy. "The Cage: Formalization, Fiduciary Duty, and Organizational Incompleteness." Working paper, 2025.

McEntire, Jeremy. "Dysmemic Pressure: Selection Dynamics in Organizational Information Environments." arXiv preprint arXiv:2512.14716, 2025.

McEntire, Jeremy. "The Mirror: Meta-Compliance and Mode B Governance." Working paper, 2025.

McEntire, Jeremy. "The Cognitive and Information-Theoretic Inevitability of Hierarchical Context Distillation." Working paper, 2025.

McEntire, Jeremy. "The Shadow Executive: Institutional Incompleteness in Military Organizations." Working paper, 2025.

Empirical Evidence

McEntire, Jeremy. "Tournament-Based Performance Evaluation and Systematic Misallocation: Why Forced Ranking Systems Produce Random Outcomes." arXiv preprint arXiv:2512.06583, 2025.

McEntire, Jeremy. "An Empirical Analysis of Linguistic Variance Compression in Post-IPO Filings." Working paper, 2025.

McEntire, Jeremy. "Jobs vs. Cook: A Quantitative Analysis of Leadership Eras at Apple." Working paper, 2025.

Structural Solutions

McEntire, Jeremy. "Internal Equity Without the Casino: A Dual-System Economy for Organizational Adaptation." Working paper, 2025.

McEntire, Jeremy. "A Graph-Theoretic Alternative to Forced Ranking." Working paper, 2025.

McEntire, Jeremy. "A Unified Theory of Management Layer Dynamics." Working paper, 2025.

McEntire, Jeremy. "The Management Layer Trap." Working paper, 2025.

Legal Foundations

McEntire, Jeremy. "The Paradox of Protection: The Business Judgment Rule and Risk Allocation." Working paper, 2025.

McEntire, Jeremy. "The Procedural Cage: Delaware Corporate Law Post-1985." Working paper, 2025.

SEC Filings Analyzed

The linguistic variance compression analysis examined S-1 and 10-K filings from the following companies. Full filing references are available in the technical paper "An Empirical Analysis of Linguistic Variance Compression in Post-IPO Filings" at cageandmirror.com.

Pre-SOX Tech Giants: Amazon (S-1: 1997; 10-K: 1997–1999), Google (S-1: 2004; 10-K: 2004–2006)

Post-SOX Enterprise SaaS: Salesforce (S-1: 2003), Workday (S-1: 2012; 10-K: 2012–2013), ServiceNow (S-1: 2012; 10-K: 2012–2013)

Consumer Internet: Netflix (S-1: 2002), Facebook/Meta (S-1: 2012; 10-K: 2012–2014), LinkedIn (S-1: 2011; 10-K: 2011–2013), Snap (S-1: 2017)

Founder-Controlled: Meta, Snap, Shopify (F-1: 2015; 40-F: 2016–2017)

High-Liability Fintech: Coinbase (S-1: 2021), Robinhood (S-1: 2021)

Born-Caged Cloud: Snowflake (S-1: 2020; 10-K/Q: 2021), Okta (S-1: 2017)

Hardware/Semiconductor: NVIDIA (S-1: 1998; 10-K: 2000), eBay (S-1: 1998; Annual Report: 1998)

Biotech: Moderna (S-1: 2018; 10-K: 2018)

Note on Citation Style: Legal cases follow standard Bluebook format. Academic works follow Chicago Manual of Style author-date conventions adapted for readability. SEC filings are referenced by form type and year; full EDGAR URLs are documented in the supporting technical papers.

Acknowledgments

This book is the product of years of observation, inquiry, and refinement. While the framework and its conclusions are mine alone, the work benefited from contributions that deserve acknowledgment.

First, to the people who inadvertently taught me the geometry of the Cage: the good bosses who modeled judgment, the bad bosses who modeled failure modes, the colleagues who showed me what invisible excellence looks like, and the teams who lived the consequences of structures they did not design.

Second, to the friends and family who tolerated the long conversations, the half-formed theories, and the obsessive pursuit of structural clarity. Their patience made sustained inquiry possible even when the work produced no visible output.

Third, to the artificial intelligence systems I used throughout this work—ChatGPT, Claude, Gemini, and Grok. They served as tireless sparring partners that surfaced contradictions, challenged assumptions, and stress-tested the framework across multiple epistemic environments. They accelerated the thinking by refusing easy answers. Any clarity here owes something to that process; the responsibility for the arguments remains entirely my own.

Finally, to the leaders who attempted to build deliberately within constraints—sometimes succeeding, sometimes failing, always teaching. Their willingness to experiment against structural gravity, to name what was broken, and to share results candidly made the Mirror more than abstraction.

This book stands on their lived experience. The responsibility for its claims stands on mine.

About the Author

Jeremy McEntire spent two decades in software and systems architecture, as chief architect and CTO. He worked inside early-stage startups, as well as larger technology environments where scale pressures expose the underlying physics of organizational behavior. These roles gave him proximity to the real mechanisms by which organizations succeed or fail.

McEntire came to organizational theory not through institutional pathways but through necessity: observing intelligent people in well-designed systems systematically degrading their own capabilities. When existing frameworks failed to explain what he saw, he began constructing his own from first principles—integrating mathematics, systems theory, corporate law, engineering practice, and empirical language analysis into a unified explanation of organizational dysfunction.

McEntire writes and consults on organizational design, leadership, and the physics of coordination at scale. His work appears at cageandmirror.com. He lives and works in Oklahoma City.

www.ingramcontent.com/pod-product-compliance
Lightning Source LLC
Chambersburg PA
CBHW030453210326
41597CB00013B/655